Hara

Contents

Hara

Illustrations

Introduction

Western ways of life have come to the end of their fruitfulness, rationalism has made its final contribution and modern
man will succumb increasingly to physical and spiritual
decay unless he finds some new way of coming back to his
essential self and the true sense of life. Even the trans-
forming and redeeming power of religion is declining in the
measure that the range of images in which it is presented
and the concept of God which it conveys have lost their
roots in man's original relation to Being. Religion today can
withstand neither rationalism nor can it satisfy man's
longing for inner safety. The predominance of the ego with
its self-centred structure of consciousness, as well as all its
claims, which obstruct and distort man's connection with
the ground of Being, is also the cause of his incapacity for
any real faith.

Faith is innate in every man thanks to the bond which
unites him with the ground of Being. It is from this
original bond that all religions spring, including the
Christian religion. But once a man is estranged from his
religion the gates of faith can re-open for him only if he
himself has an experience of the divine ground of Being, for
the hidden treasure of all mankind is there, before any
interpretation of it and beyond any confession. So the way
to real faith, even for the Christian who has possessed only
a pseudo-faith and who has finally foundered on a rationalistic concept of God, lies through an intimate experience
of Being which will renew his feeling-contact with the
divine ground, as well as form in him an inner attitude
which will permit him to take this experience seriously and
to prove it in his daily life. The search for ways to gain this
new experience of Being, and an attitude appropriate to it,
is the urgent task facing us today.

The break-through to Being as well as the transformation

11

arising from the sense of oneness with the divine ground is imperative today for all those who are standing on the 'front line' of the spirit.

The realizing of the possibility of a living faith rests, like faith of all ages, on three pillars—experience, insight and practice. Our task today is to help the man who has come to the end of his tether, by revealing to him the latent content of his deepest and most essential experiences, by opening the door to the basic truths and laws of life, and above all by showing him a way to achieve by practice a lasting attitude in consonance with them, without which there can be no progress in faith and no inner ripening.

One way of approaching this task lies through the discovery of Hara. By Hara—and we hold to this name—the Japanese understand an all-inclusive general attitude which enables a man to open himself to the power and wholeness of the original life-force and to testify to it by the fulfilment, the meaningfulness and the mastery displayed in his own life. Knowledge of Hara is valid not only for the Japanese. It has universal human validity. The purpose of this book is to lead the reader to the essence and meaning of Hara. It is directed not only to professional therapists and medical men but to everyone who is a seeker, or a teacher or who is entrusted in any way with the shaping and education of others. The theoretical analysis of Hara, as well as its practice in the service of self-development, touch at every point on problems dealt with daily by spiritual advisers and professional psychologists. It may therefore be useful to make some remarks on how Hara relates to present day psychology and psycho-therapy.

It becomes clearer and clearer that every neurosis conceals a universal human problem—the problem of ripening. In its deepest sense ripening means the same thing both for the sound and the unsound, that is, the progressive integration of the individual with his being, his essence, wherein he takes part in the great Being. For the neurotic the possibility of finding his essence is merely obstructed in a peculiar way because of his substitution mechanisms.

Immaturity, unripeness, is the cancer of our time, the incapacity to ripen the specific mark of our time. The neurosis which drives the spiritually sick to the therapist is simply the clearest expression of the universal suffering, the suffering due to man's estrangement from Being! The specific symptoms of such suffering are, in all cases, stopping points and blind alleys on the return to Being. Healthy and unhealthy alike are to be understood as 'on the way'— hence never statically, but always in the perspective of their becoming one with their being. So it comes to this, that as in the East since time immemorial between pupil and master, so today between a sound person and his spiritual counsellor, between a 'disturbed' person and his therapist—all are seeking, over and above any psychological aid, a firm metaphysical foundation for life. A longing from their being moves them all. They seek resonance and guidance out of a need which is not only constitutional and personal but which involves their whole existence. Such need requires more than 'psychology'.

Modern man suffers from his immaturity and causes suffering to all around him. What we are called upon to do is to retore him to the context of the Greater Life, to unblock the door to at-one-ment with the wellsprings of his existence, and to show him the way to give expression to his contact with Being through a life-affirming attitude. For there is a *way* to be trodden by actual practice. In the effort to comprehend this way—on which man can rediscover and strengthen his roots in the ground of being —teachers and spiritual counsellors to the healthy must join hands with those who tend the mentally sick. To such a collaboration this book is dedicated.

I
Hara in the Life of the Japanese

Chapter 1

Hara in the Life of the Japanese

' "Chest out—belly in" . . . a nation capable of taking this injunction as a general rule is in great danger,' said a Japanese to me in 1938. It was during my first visit to Japan. I did not understand this sentence then. Today I know it is true, and why.

'Chest out—belly in' is the shortest formula for expressing an attitude which is wrong in principle, to be more precise, a wrong bodily attitude which prompts and fixes a wrong mental attitude. What does this mean? That a man should stand or sit bent over or stooped or slumped together? Certainly not, but straight and erect. 'Chest out —belly in' however leads to a posture which just misses the natural structure of the human body. Where the centre of gravity shifts upward to the chest and the middle of the body is gainsaid and constricted the natural alternation of tension and relaxation is replaced by a wrong one which forces a man to swing between hypertension and slackness.

But how can this become 'a danger to the nation'? Because this wrong posture both expresses and consolidates a false ordering of the inner forces which prevents their true order, for where everything is drawn upward there is no right centring. But is not the heart the natural centre of man? And is not man the being destined either to lift himself heavenwards and to master his life with his 'head' and 'will', or failing this, to accept and endure it with his heart? Certainly he is. But right mastery and the strength to endure will be achieved only when the forces located in the upper part of his body and their centre, the ego, operate not independently and separately but are constantly held in check and guided by those that lie at a deeper level.

Man, *as a living being*, is not rooted in himself. Rather is he nourished, sustained and held in order by Nature whose laws operate without his knowledge and assistance. Man sets himself in opposition to the order of life which fundamentally sustains him if, by an unnatural shifting of his centre of gravity, he denies that vital centre in his bearing which testifies to this order.

Intellect, will and emotion, the powers of head, chest and heart with which man as a conscious being has been endowed will prove his undoing if, caught in the net of his concepts, in the brilliance of his achievements and in the web of his entanglements he forgets his anchorage in the weaving and working of the Greater Life. Just as the growth and un- folding of the crown of a tree depends directly on its root-system, so also the vital development of man's spirit depends on his being true to his roots, that is, to an un- interrupted contact with the primal unity of Life, from which human life also springs. If, forgetting this, man diminishes the realm of his primal life by artificially pulling himself upwards physically he disturbs the balance of his natural forces, and the inflated I then bars access to that higher development which it is its real function humbly to prepare, protect and serve.

The ego as the centre of our natural consciousness can serve the true meaning of all human life only if instead of posing as master, it remains the servant of the Greater Life. Where 'chest out—belly in' is the maxim the little ego ascends the throne and it is this arrogant assumption of the I which is 'the danger to the nation'. Fundamentally we in the West are also aware of this danger, as the East has been since time immemorial. But the East, never having been as cut off from contact with the basic vital centre as we are, and being more perceptive than we, is still able to hear its warning voice at times when emotion, intellect or will endanger the contact with the primordial source of Life. The East heeds its warning to man ever to remember his origins, knows the secret of how to regain contact with it when temporarily it is lost and obeys the command not to lose contact with it as consciousness increases, in fact to cherish it then more than ever. Only thus can man consciously become more and more what, as mere nature and unconsciously, he already is: a child of the all-embracing divine unity of Life wherein his own life is rooted, and in which unconsciously and with longing he is constantly seeking his true centre whenever, as an intellectually developed being, he has debarred himself from it. The Japanese term Hara means nothing other than the physical embodiment of the original Life centre in man.

Man is originally endowed and invested with Hara. But when, as a rational being, he loses what is embodied in Hara it becomes his *task* to regain it. To rediscover the unity concealed in the contradictions through which he perceives life intellectually is the nerve of his existence. As a rational being he feels himself suspended between the opposite poles of heaven and earth, spirit and nature. This means first the dichotomy of unconscious nature and of the mind which urges him to ever-increasing consciousness; and second, the dichotomy of his time-space reality on this earth and the Divine beyond time and space. Man's whole existence is influenced by the tormenting tension of these opposites and so he is forever in search of a life-form in which this tension will be resolved.

What is man to do when he feels himself suspended between two opposing poles? He can surrender himself to the one or to the other and so, for a time disavow the contradition; or he can seek a third way in which it will be resolved. The only right choice is the one which will not endanger the wholeness of his being. Since man in his wholeness must include both poles his salvation lies only in choosing the way which unifies them. For man is destined to manifest anew the unity of life within all the contradictions of his existence. The way to this unity is long. The integration of these two poles—the unconscious, and the conscious life of the mind, as well as between life in space time reality and the Reality beyond space time—constitutes the way to human maturity. Maturity is that condition in which man reaps the fruit of the union he has regained. The realization of this union means that he has found his true vital centre. Basis, symbol and proof of this is the presence of.

These few indications already show that Hara is of universal concern. And although the term Hara is of Japanese origin it is still valid for all mankind. Just as Eastern wisdom cannot be exclusive to the East but must be valid for all humanity (the East having striven for it more persistently than we) so this flower of Eastern wisdom concerns the West no less than the East, and not only in theory but in practice as well. What is meant by Eastern wisdom is never a mere condensation of theoretical knowledge but the fruit of ripe experience, confirmed and proved by faithful, patient practice. We can grasp the full meaning of Hara only if we look into the experiences which have led to its conception and indicate the exercises which form it.

Hara is that state (*Verfassung*) in which the individual has found his primal centre, and has proven himself by it. When we speak of the state of an individual we mean something that concerns him in his entirety, that is, something that transcends the duality of body and soul. But because man is a unity of body and soul—the body, as Ludwig Klages says, being the outward form of the soul and the soul the inner import of the body—the structure of the whole individual is necessarily made apparent and legible in the form and order of his body. There is no psychic structure and no inner tension which is not reflected in the body. Hence the discovery of the inner psychological centre implies also the discovery of the physical centre.

But where is the centre of the body? In the region of the navel, or, to be precise, a little below the navel. Therefore it should not surprise us that Hara, the essence of the vital centre literally translated means belly. That the physical centre of gravity of a man who has found his equilibrium should be located in his belly sounds strange to European ears. Why the strengthened belly should be the symbol of the vital centre regained will now be shown by examples from everyday life in Japan.

Chapter 2

Hara in the Everyday Life of Japan

Whoever gives a lecture to a Japanese audience for the first time may meet with an experience as unexpected as it is unpleasant. The audience, it seems, gradually goes to sleep. This was what happened to me. It was bewildering. The more urgently I talked, the more desperately I tried to save the situation, the more my listeners closed their eyes until finally, so it seemed to me, half the room was blissfully asleep. But when without the least emphasis I uttered the word *Tenno*, Emperor, all were suddenly wide awake as if struck by lightning and gazed at me with wide open and not in the least sleepy eyes. They had not slept after all. Turned in on themselves, they had been attentive in their own way and I had overlooked the fact that although their eyes were closed they had been sitting erect and controlled.

Every stranger in Japan is struck at first by the sight of people apparently asleep and submerged in themselves. In trams and trains everywhere one sees men and women, even young people, girls and students sitting with closed or half closed eyes but erect and completely still. When they open their eyes they do not look in the least sleepy, on the contrary, their glance seems to arise from deep below, completely tranquil and present, from which the world with its turbulent diversity seems to rebound. It is a look which shows that the individual is completely collected and unperturbed, awake but not over-responsive, controlled yet not rigid.

A Japanese sitting on a chair or a bench looks very often as though he were resting in himself rather than on the furniture. The way in which a Japanese sits down on a chair shows the degree of his Westernization. Crossing the legs and so throwing the small of the back out of line and compressing the abdomen is entirely un-Japanese and so is any leaning or lolling position which would eliminate the supporting strength of the back. The Japanese, to whichever class he may belong, holds himself erect and 'in form' even when sitting. That this custom is weakening today through the increasing influence of the West is doubtless true—but this is a deviation from the traditional essentially Japanese form which alone concerns us here.

The foregoing examples show two things. The Japanese way of sitting is connected with an inner as well as an outer attitude. The Japanese rests upright and composed within himself. This combination of uprightness and resting within oneself is typical. The whole person is, as it were, gathered inward.

Another striking example of significant posture is the one that a Japanese assumes in front of the camera. The European is often surprised at how much the posture of important public men, such as high ranking army officers or newly elected Cabinet members, differs from that of Europeans when being photographed. Whereas the latter take great pains to stand 'at ease' or 'with nonchalance', or 'with dignity', shoulders drawn up and chest thrust forward, the Japanese stand quite differently, often, to our eyes, with deliberate ungainliness—unassumingly front face with loose hung shoulders and arms but still upright and firm, the legs slightly apart. Never does the Japanese stand with his weight on the one leg while the other 'idles'. Anyone standing in this way, without centre, without axis, inspires little confidence in a Japanese.

I remember a large reception, the guests European and Japanese, stood around after dinner drinking coffee and smoking. A Japanese friend of mine who knew of my interest in the ways of his country joined me and said, 'Do you see that the Europeans standing here could be easily toppled over if one were suddenly to give them a little push from behind? But none of the Japanese would lose their balance even if they were given a much harder push.'

How is this stability achieved? The bodily centre of gravity is not drawn upward but held firmly in the middle, in the region of the navel. And that is the point. The belly is not pulled in but free—and yet slightly tensed. The shoulder region instead of being tense is relaxed but the trunk is firm. The upright bearing is not a pulling upwards but is the manifestation of an axis which stands firmly on a reliable base and which by its own strength maintains its uprightness. Whether a person is corpulent or thin is immaterial.

Upright, firm and collected—these are the three marks of that posture which is typical of the Japanese who knows how to stand, and taken altogether, show the presence of Hara.

This Hara as the basis of posture is no less noticeable in women than in men. Only that the posture of women as observed in the street by the foreigner, where at first he mainly encounters them, is different in some ways—the look of being self-enclosed, of deep inner collectedness is so emphasized as to suggest self-absorption. The Japanese woman emphasizes an attitude which is completely opposed to that of the pre-potent, more expanding attitude of the Western woman. 'As far as possible, not to be in evidence. To move, taking up as little space as possible. To be as though one were not there at all!'. As a result of such an inner disposition the women keep their arms pressed close to their sides, never swinging, heads slightly bent, shoulders dropped and a little pulled in, and when walking they trip along with knees scarcely separated, toes turned in and taking very small steps. The stronger the influence of tradition on the Japanese woman the more grotesque appears to her the walk of the European or American. What strikes us as especially free and at ease seems to the Japanese woman unfeminine and insolent, quasi-masculine, immodest and above all naïve—for all this expresses an inner attitude of self-assurance which takes life altogether too much for granted.

Man in his self-assurance holds too strongly to what he believes is his by his own efforts. Not only does he not hesitate to attract attention to himself but he even emphasizes his 'persona'. This means that he lacks the wise restraint suitable both in social life and towards those greater forces which are present everywhere and which may suddenly fall on him and attack him. Vis-à-vis these forces man is better prepared either to ward them off or deliberately to let them in, if the deep-centredness of the soul-body posture at least counter-balances the outward thrust and striving of the mind or, better still, slightly preponderates over it. When circumstances oblige a Japanese to show himself in public, for instance, when 'the man at the top' has to put himself forward because his office requires him to do so, or when the Headmaster of a school has to go on the platform and deliver the speech of the day, one can observe the most astonishing movements of withdrawal such a man makes when he steps down from the platform— movements which have only one intention, that is, to demonstrate that he knows that 'one must make a personal withdrawal in the same degree as one's function required one to put oneself forward'. Hence the embarrassment, sense of shame even which a Japanese gathering feels for a European making a speech, for example if in any way he 'shows off' Such behaviour, so often repeated by our Western representatives in Japan, alienates sympathy far more than we suspect. For avoiding all postures emphasizing the ego the Japanese has one sure remedy—his firm Hara.

Hara

The sitting-still of the Japanese, especially of the Japanese woman, this completely motionless and yet inwardly alert sitting still, has baffled many a foreigner. Most Westerners have their first opportunity of observing at close range the ways of Japanese women in the tea houses where the serving girls and the geishas are called in to grace an evening. What is most impressive is very often their way of sitting still—knees together, resting on their heels, withdrawn into themselves and yet completely free and relaxed. If with a swift and supple motion they rise from this position to do something such as pouring out the rice wine, they return immediately and without loss of poise to the quiet sitting posture, upright and attentive, completely there, yet not there at all, and just wait until the next thing has to be done. In the same way in her own home the mistress of the house sits by modestly while the men talk, but so also sits the ballad singer, and the singing geisha, and so sits the male choir in the Kabuki, the classical theatre, and so the Samurai—so they all sit and so they stand like symbols of life, collected and ready for anything. And as they sit and stand so also do they walk and dance and wrestle and fence, fundamentally motionless. For every movement is as though anchored in an immovable centre from which all motion flows and from which it receives its force, direction and measure. The immovable centre lies in Hara.

The spirit which determines the fundamental attitudes of the Japanese finds the realm of its practice and preservation in the temples. Evidence of this is the posture of the monk in meditation. He demonstrates the attitude-posture in which alone a man can become 'the right vessel'—opened in the right way and closed in the right way, ready to receive and preserve. The figure of the monk in meditation taken generally as the pattern of religious feeling is much more present to the Japanese, even in their everyday postures, than the posture of the priest in prayer is to us. The bodily attitude of the monk as he opens himself to the

Divine in the desire to become one with it is also the posture which the people, in so far as the great spiritual tradition is still alive in them, know as the one which should never be lost. They realize that life on earth both in its need and in its fulfilment can be rightly achieved only if a man does not fall out of the cosmic order and if he maintains his contact with the great original Unity. Enduring contact with it is shown by the man who keeps his unshakeable centre of gravity in that centre which is Hara.

It is evident that the image of the monk in meditation which lives in the people as a kind of posture-consciousness is not regarded as a dreary or oppressive ideal, exaggerated or imposed from above, but as the perfected expression of man's transformation through that Great Experience which re-unites him with his true origin. The knowledge that this experience is a practicable, attainable possibility for every-one remains a universal possession of all Eastern peoples. To the man who has not yet had it, it exists as a fore-knowledge, full of promise and implying an obligation.

Thus we have to accept, although not without a sense of shame, that in the everyday life of the Japanese the bells of eternity are, so to speak, always ringing. From the temple gongs there echoes in a sublime form the admonishing voice which, like a counterpoint giving meaning to all the sounds of daily life, unceasingly resounds within. Thus also the calm bearing of the meditating monk reminds men that to suffer from life shows only estrangement from life. The Japanese is generally aware of what is at stake fundamentally, not through intellectual concepts but from intimations brought by experience; and the images before which he prays are for him symbols and sources of the strength which he finds in the great Reality. For him, as distinct from the Westerner, origin and goal are both contained in the experience of this Reality.

The most impressive representation of the Hara attitude is found in the figures of the Buddha who, in the 'Great

27

Experience' is completely fused with the Absolute. The Buddha statues are symbols of that state of the soul which man is called upon to manifest in his body where origin, meaning and goal of life have become one. The pictures and statues of the Buddha clearly show the centre of gravity in the centre of the body. We find this emphasis on the centre in the pictures of the Buddha sitting in deep meditation, his hands resting on his crossed legs, as well as in those where he stands upright with raised hands. We can see it in the pictures of the Boddhisattvis as well in those of Kwannon, the symbol of compassion and loving kindness. Emphasis on the centre of the body has nothing to do with corpulence. The slender figures of the earlier periods also show the centre of gravity in the lower abdomen.

The posture of the monk in meditation represents something fundamentally right and as such binding for all. The same applies to the Buddha image. It is not something unattainable for the ordinary person. These images only symbolize the complete achievement of what is in principle possible for everyone. This is because basically everyone *is* what the Buddha expresses, and, in the course of his development, can become it in so far as he will allow it to manifest. But only by practice and application can the state of being revealed in the Buddha effigy be achieved wherein the devotee beholds his own possibilities. A Buddha is not a transcendental god, but a human being into whom the Great Being has penetrated bringing transformation and liberation into the bright light of consciousness. And in his form is the reflection of what, from the beginning, is given to every man to rediscover at-homeness in the Centre of Being.

Just as we see in the Buddha effigies the emphasis on the centre of gravity in the lower body we find it again in the representations of mythological figures and of sages. We find it in the pictures of the great leaders, of the popular gods of good luck and in the many illustrations of Boddhidharma, the blue-eyed monk who brought Zen Buddhism to China and became famous for his imperturbable 'sitting'. His image is still given to children as a tumbler doll with a round, lead-weighted belly which always brings him back to his upright position no matter how often he is knocked down.

It follows as a matter of course that an understanding of the importance of the body-soul centre has influenced the Japanese ideal of beauty. It is characteristic that their 'beauty' should be different from ours. In our ideal we see beauty in the symmetry and perfect form of the body. We look for perfection and harmony of the whole and its parts. It is undoubtedly true that this ideal was originally determined by the idea of the unity of body and soul. Today, however, the popular concept of beauty as compared with this ideal has become largely superficial and externalized, and the culture of the body informed by the spirit has been replaced by a cult of the well proportioned body accentuating the erotic in the woman and the virile and masculine in the man. The more discriminating man on the other hand caring less for this merely physical beauty finds it in the expression of the soul beside which the beauty of the outward form has but little importance. Thus the Western ideal of beauty alternates in a typical way between the opposite poles of body and soul. This dichotomy plays no part in the mind of the Japanese. He regards as beautiful the figure which represents a being well grounded in his basic centre.

For this and no other reason he values a certain emphasis on the belly, and the reserved bearing which is evidence of its firmness. It is not surprising therefore that a bridegroom, if he is too thin, tries to acquire a little belly in order to please his bride and also that the strong belly (provided it emphasizes the right centre of gravity—not to be confused with the blown-out stomach) is considered attractive and not repulsive as in the West. Indeed the idols of the people, the *sumo* masters (*sumo* is Japanese wrestling) often have enormous bellies and yet, despite their weight incredible nimbleness, a cat-like agility and elasticity. The seat of their strength is in their belly, not merely physical strength as is revealed in their often immensely developed muscles but also of a supernatural strength. They demonstrate in a spectacular way what made them masters quite apart from their technical skill—they really demonstrate Hara.

If a man has Hara he no longer needs any physical strength at all, he wins through a quite different kind of strength. I had the opportunity to watch an impressive example of this during the last elimination round of a *sumo* championship.

Breathlessly awaited by thousands of spectators, two masters entered the ring at the Koguki-Kan in Tokyo. With great dignity each one in turn steps out of his corner, casts consecrated rice into the ring, goes with legs wide apart into a full knee bend, then stamps mightily first with one foot then with the other. After a ceremonious bow they approach each other, squat down with hands on the ground and gaze at each other eye to eye. Then both wrestlers spring up from this position—but not before both have inwardly assented to the start of the contest. If one of them while they have been eyeing each other closes his eyelids it means 'I am not yet ready'. And as the contest can begin only when each one is 'in form' this is a signal for them both to stand up, separate, and again squat facing each other until both are finally fully ready. The umpire who has watched everything closely gives the sign and off they go. Both wrestlers leap into the air and the crowd is prepared to see a mighty battle.

But what happens? One, after a short struggle, simply raises his hand, on which the hand of the other lies flat, and, as if he were dealing with a puppet he pushes his opponent almost without touching him and without the use of any visible effort, slowly and softly out of the ring. He wins in the true sense, without fighting. The defeated wrestler falls backwards over the ropes and the multitude goes mad with excitement while everything that is not nailed down is hurled into the air and rains down upon the victor from all sides in tribute to his prowess. That was Hara, demonstrated by a master. And as such it was applauded by the crowd.

This example shows very clearly that in Hara there is a supernatural force which makes possible extraordinary natural achievement in the world. And as Hara is ever present to the Japanese as the sign of a matured inwardness he also knows about it as a mysterious power which can produce super-normal results. From childhood the Japanese is taught the power of Hara. *Hara, Hara,* the father calls to the growing boy when he seems to fail in a task or when physical pain saps his morale and threatens to over-power him or when he loses his head with excitement. This Hara, Hara, however, implies and produces something different from our 'pull yourself together'. With Hara one remains balanced both in action and in endurance. All this is such a natural, basic and general knowledge for the Japanese that it is not at all easy for him if you ask him about his secret treasure to raise it to consciousness, let alone to explain it.

Another typical example from the war. Not only is the training of the soldier as a matter of course a training in Hara but the civilian population also found in Hara the strength to endure all perils. When the leader of the Japanese Women's Associations on her return from a visit to Germany, spoke in a lecture of the impressive air-raid precautions she had seen there, she added 'we have nothing of all that but we have something else, we have Hara'. The interpreter was greatly embarrassed. How should he trans-late that? What could he do but simply say 'belly'? Silence, laughter. Only a few of the Westerners understood what was meant, but the Japanese knew that the lecturer had quite simply meant that power which, even if it gave no protection against annihilation by bombs, yet made possible an inner calm from which springs the greatest possible presence of mind and the greatest possible capacity for endurance.

He who has Hara can be prepared for anything and everything, even for death, and keep calm in any situation. He can even bow to the victor without loss of dignity and he can wait. He does not resist the turning wheel of fate but calmly bides his time. With Hara the world looks different, it is as it is, always different from what one wants it to be and yet always in harmony. Self-will causes suffering. Suffering denotes deviation from the Great Unity and reveals the truth of the Whole. The ordinary eye does not see this—the Hara sense apprehends it and only when will, feeling and intellect are 'comprehended' in Hara do they cease to resist what is, and instead, through it, serve the 'way' in which all things are contained. To discover that way, to recognize it and thereafter never to lose it is tantamount to genuine striving for Hara.

Chapter 3

Hara as the Purpose of Practice

Hara, it is true, is part of man's original endowment but, for that very reason, poses a task for him—for it is the task of man to become what he is. Man can fulfil his task of becoming a complete human being only if he overcomes again and again that within him which obstructs the way to this true becoming, and also if, at the same time, he apprehends and allows to grow within him that basic power which is always striving to carry him on to his fully human state.

The task of gaining the right basic centre can be fulfilled only by one who, with perseverance and sincerity, without fear of pain and with great patience, overcomes whatever hinders Hara, and furthers that which the developed Hara expresses. To become a complete human being without acquiring the body-soul 'centre' is not possible. But to acquire Hara through practice means also opening the gate to the way by which Man can become *whole*.

Only that individual is truly 'whole' whose self manifests the Being[1] embodied within him. A man is not 'whole' as

[1] By 'Being' (*Wesen*) is meant here the individual manner of participation in that Being which transcends time and space. 'Self' means here the subjective existence in time and space. The 'True Self' is attained when a man's subjective existence is integrated with Being. Where this is not the case man's self (e.g. the 'I' in its relation to the world) is a 'pseudo-self'. In the True Self man's participation in Being manifests as freedom in the world of time and space; the self-awareness of the 'I' is dependent on the world.

long as he fails to accomplish his integration with Being, as long as, for example, he lives only in the I that is not conformable with Being, but activated always from without. For Western Man the realisation of Being within the self is inevitably connected with the unfolding of the perceiving and creative mind. But this unfolding also presupposes his re-rooting in the primal centre, which is Hara.

We in the West have over-valued achievement; the East has under-valued it, and today is determined to make up for this neglect by taking lessons from the Western countries and striving as never before to acquire the theoretical and practical knowledge necessary for mastering life on this earth. Of these things which the East has hitherto lacked we have too much. But of those things—notably the Inner Way —which the East has cultivated from time immemorial, we know as yet all too little. Therefore where the inner way is concerned we can take lessons from the East. And because Hara, as understood by the Japanese, leads to inner *maturity*, the practice of it is of special importance for the West.

By practice the Japanese mean something different from what we mean. When we hear the word 'practice' we think of doing something which will give us skill, what the Americans call know-how. A skill enabling us *to do* or *to produce* something properly. 'Practice makes perfect' or 'Practice makes the master' as the German saying has it. But who is a master in the accepted meaning of this term? A master is one who so masters his craft that the perfect result is guaranteed. Such skill presupposes long practice. Only persistent practice leads to real ability and only real ability produces the perfect *result*, in deed or in work.

Every form of activity can, according to the degree of skill on which it is based, be more or less perfect, that is 'masterly'. This applies to all forms of sport and to all the activities of our daily lives. It is one of our errors to see the possibility of mastery only in achievements which presuppose a specific talent and which call for a specific training. In fact, however, every action which is repeated again and again conceals the possibility of inner perfection, making him who achieves it master of this action. In this sense 'masterly' walking, running, speaking, writing and much else is possible, and also the masterly practice of a sport, which however has nothing to do with that degradation of the idea of mastery which produces a mania for record-breaking. And so there exists the masterly command of innumerable actions, even small unimportant ones, which are repeated a thousand times a day, at home and at work, in the office and in social life, as well as the mastery of special actions.

In this inner work more is involved than the accomplishment of an outward action. Inner work is concerned with what outlasts the finished outward action. It fulfils itself in a form which 'stands alone' because it stands perfected in itself. A masterpiece is valid because nothing can be added to, nothing taken away from it. Every detail is necessary because demanded by the whole. Like the perfectly performed action, perfected work also presupposes the greatest skill and this in turn presupposes practice. Only long practice resulting in the great skill reveals the master of the perfect work. But in outward action and inner work alike the meaning of practice, so understood, is revealed by what comes out of it.

One speaks of a 'master'—whether of an outer action or inner work—only when success is achieved not only now and then, but with absolute certainty. Certainty of success presupposes more than perfected skill alone. What is this more? It is the state or condition of the performer which makes his performance infallible. However well-performed an action may be, however well controlled a technique, as long as the man using it is subject to moods and atmosphere, unrelaxed and easily disturbed, for example, when he is being watched, then he is a master only in a very limited degree. He is master only of technique and not of himself. He controls the skill he has but not what he is in himself. And if a man can do more than he *is* his skill often fails him in critical moments. Real control over oneself can only be achieved by a special training, the outcome of which is not just technical skill, but an established frame of mind (*Verfassung*) which *ensures* the required result.

This is *practice* understood as exercise (exercitium). Its purpose is not an outer visible result but an inner achievement. In practice of this kind the person developing, not the deed or the visible work as such, is what matters. And as surely as genuine mastery of performance or skill presupposes a certain personal inner quality so, conversely, the preparing of oneself for performance or skill can be used as a way leading to inner mastery.

In this way the meaning of achieving outward and applied skill is transposed to the inner life. More important than outward success then is that personal quality which will, when developed produce not only the perfect external result, but which will have its real meaning and value within itself.

Understood thus, every art, every skill can become an opportunity to develop 'on the inner way', and so a saying of the Japanese becomes understandable; 'Archery and dancing, flower-arranging and singing, tea-drinking and wrestling—it is all *the same.*'[1] From the viewpoint of performance of 'work', this saying does not make sense, but once its underlying significance has been grasped—man's true self-becoming—then its meaning is clear.

For the Japanese[2] every art as well as every sport has a purpose beyond mere outward achievement. In practising it he aims at that quality of the whole man which produces results that appear to be casual, unintentional, without

---

[1] See *Japan and the Cult of Tranquillity*. Rider.
[2] 'The Japanese' here always means not any Japanese, but one who embodies the national tradition.

conscious effort—just as an apple, when ripe, drops from the tree without any help from the tree.

At the core of this attitude (*Verfassung*) is the imperturbility of the centre of gravity in the true centre which is Hara. I still remember my amazement when, in my early efforts to penetrate into the nature of the various Japanese 'master practises' first in talks with masters of their arts, I heard again and again the word *Hara* pronounced with particular emphasis. Whether I talked to a master of swordsmanship, of dancing, of puppetry, of painting or of any other art, he invariably concluded his exposition of the relevant training by emphasizing Hara as the cardinal point of all effort. Thus I soon realized that this word obviously meant *more* than a mere pre-requisite for the unfailing exercise of any technique. Hara seemed to be connected with something fundamental, something ultimate.

My last doubts were removed by the answer of a Japanese General when I asked him what part Hara played in the training of the soldier. The General, at first surprised at being asked this question by a European, hesitated a moment, then said quite simply: 'The meaning of all military training *is Hara*.' A surprising sentence, comprehensible only if Hara is taken as the establishment of an inner condition which makes the achievement of a given skill no less than that of the soldierly virtue of facing every circumstance—even and especially death—a simple, unemotional matter of course.

Such a condition presupposes liberation from the domination of an 'I' which fears death, and this again is possible only when a man is anchored in the ground of Being which, as the Japanese say, 'lies beyond life and death'. The inner transformation of man as the sense and purpose of practice may be illustrated by the following:

It was a hot summer day in Tokyo and I was waiting for Master Kenran Umeji, my instructor in Archery. For some weeks I had been practising on my own and was looking forward to showing the master that I had learned my lesson. I was eager to see what surprise the day's lesson would bring, for every time the master came something unexpected happened.

The learning of a Japanese art—be it archery or swords-manship, flower-arrangement or painting, calligraphy or the art of drinking tea—holds many curious experiences for the Western aspirant. If, for instance, he supposes that the chief thing in archery is to hit the target, he is much mistaken. But what then? Well, this was brought home to me very clearly that day.

The master arrived at the appointed time—a short talk over a cup of tea—and then we proceeded into the garden where the target stood. This target brought me the first surprise of many that awaited me. It was a bundle of straw about three feet across, placed at eye level on a wooden stand, my feelings may be imagined when I was told that a pupil had to practice two or three years before this target and, what is more, at a distance of about three yards. To aim for three years at a wide straw bundle from a distance of three yards! Wouldn't that be boring? It proved quite the contrary. The more one realizes the purpose of the practice the more exciting it becomes; because the problem of hitting the target never arises. What then? Well, today I was going to find out.

I take up my position. The master stands before me. As custom demands I bow low first to him and then, turning left, to the target, face the master again and calmly carry out the first movements. Each movement must flow smoothly from the previous one. I place the bow on my left knee, take up one of the arrows resting against my right leg, place it on the string; the left hand holds arrow and bow firmly together—and then the right is slowly raised, only to be lowered again while the breath flows out completely. The hand grasps the string and then—slowly breathing in— the bow is gradually drawn while being raised. This is the decisive movement which must be carried out as calmly and steadily as the moon rises in the evening sky. Before I have even reached the point where the arrow must touch the ear and cheek, and the whole bow is stretched to its fullest capacity, the deep voice of the master cuts right through me, 'Stop!' Surprised and a little irritated because of this interruption at the moment of utmost concentration, I lower the bow. The master takes it from my hands, winds the string once round the end of the bow and hands it back to me smiling. 'Once again, please.' Unsuspecting, I begin again to go through the same series of motions. But when it comes to drawing the bow my strength fails me. The bow has now *twice* the tension it had before and my strength is insufficient. My arms begin to tremble, I sway unsteadily to and fro, the posture so painstakingly won is lost. The master, however, begins to laugh. Desperately I try again, but it is hopeless. Nothing but a pitiful failure. I must have looked rather vexed for the master asks: 'What are you so annoyed about?' 'What? You can ask me that? For weeks and weeks I have practised and now, at the vital moment, you interrupt me before I have even drawn.' Once again the master laughs cheerfully, then suddenly serious, he says something like this: 'What exactly do you want? That you had accomplished the task I had given you I could see from the way you took up your bow. But the point is this—when a man, perhaps after a long struggle, has achieved a certain form in himself, in his life, in his work, only one misfortune can then befall him—that fate should allow him to stand still in that achievement. If fate means well by him it knocks his success out of his hands before it sets and hardens. To do just this during practice is the task of the good teacher. For what is the point of all this? Not the hitting of the target. For what ultimately matters, in learning archery or any other art, is not what comes out of it but what goes *into* it. Into, that is *into* the person. The self-practice in the service of an outward accomplishment serves, beyond it, the development of the inner man. And what endangers this inner development more than anything else? Standing still in his achievement. A man must go on increasing, endlessly increasing.'

The master's voice had grown grave now and urgent, and indeed, this kind of archery is something quite different from the enjoyable sport where one competes with friends in hitting a target. It is a school of life—or to use a modern expression, an existential practice.

At the beginning it is, of course, necessary to acquire the outward technique. But when the outward form is mastered, the real work begins, the unflagging work on oneself. The art of archery, like any other art for the Japanese, is an opportunity of penetrating the depth of his being. It can be achieved only by the arduous process of refining out the vain and ambitious I which, precisely because it is so eager for outward success, endangers success. When this I is transcended success will come—achieved, not through the outer skill directed by an ambitious will, but through a new inner Being. It will be due then to a condition in which a deeper, one could say, a supernatural strength is released in us achieving, without our assistance as it were, the perfect result.

In this way we can understand the words of an old Japanese whose opinion I asked concerning the miracles of the Indian Yogis. He said: 'Certainly a man who has devoted years or decades to the development of certain faculties can produce results which seem miraculous to the untrained. But the question is, what is the value of such achievements? If they are nothing but the result of a technique acquired from motives of pride they have no importance. Only when they give evidence of *inner* mastery are they of value.'

Such were the words of the old Japanese—surprising words for us Europeans who idolize achievement for its own sake. In the East, what is considered masterly is only that which proves inner *maturity*, which produces ripe fruit as a tree does, effortlessly. The way it works out in practice can be shown by an experience I once had during a visit to a Japanese monastery.

It was in Kyoto in 1941. A Japanese friend had arranged for me to meet Master Hayashi, the abbot of the famous Zen monastery, Myoshinji. In Japan they observe the charming custom of giving gifts. The guest brings the host a gift when visiting him for the first time and never departs without receiving one in return. A gift one has made oneself is valued most. And so, when, after a good long talk, it was time for me to go, Master Hayashi said: 'I should like to give you something. I will paint something for you.' Two younger monks fetched painting materials. A red cloth was spread on the mats, an extremely thin sheet of rice-paper measuring about 60 by 20 cm. was laid on it and held in place by two lead weights to prevent it from slipping. Then brush and ink were brought in—not ink ready for use, but solid ink which has to be rubbed in a hollowed out stone and made liquid by the addition of water.

Relaxed and calm, as if he had infinite time—and a Master always has infinite inner time—the abbot began to prepare the ink. To and fro, to and fro his hand moved until gradually the water had turned into liquid black. I wondered that the master did this task himself and asked why no one did it for him. The answer was significant: 'The steady movement of the hand carefully preparing the ink makes one completely calm. Everything becomes still inside. Only from an undisturbed, quiet heart can something perfect flower.' Now everything was ready.

Master Hayashi knelt on the floor, that is, he sat upright on his heels, his brow serene and his shoulders loose with that freedom of the upper body which is supported by strength from below, and which is characteristic of those practised in sitting. With an inimitably calm and at the same time fluid movement the master took up the brush.

For a moment his eyes rested almost as if lost on the paper and then it seemed as if he completely freed himself inwardly so as to let the picture within emerge unimpeded, quite free of any fear that it might fail, or any personal determination that it had to succeed. And so it emerged.

With sure strokes there appeared a picture of Kwannon, the goddess of Mercy. First the face, with a few delicate strokes, then the flowing robe with more vigorous strokes and the petals of the lotus flower on which she sat, and then, *then* came the moment for the sake of which I am telling this story: the drawing of the halo surrounding the head of Kwannon, that is, the free-hand drawing of the perfect circle. All of us present held our breath, because the masterly demonstration of ultimate composure—the proof of sovereign freedom from all fear in the perfect action that executes itself—is always a gripping experience. It must be noted that any hesitation, any flicker of the brush produces a smudge on the skin thin paper which would spoil everything. But, without hesitating for a single moment, the master dipped his brush into the ink, wiped it a little, placed it on the paper and, as if it were the easiest thing in the world, he wrote, as it were, the perfect circle, which like an emanation of divine purity, surrounded the head of Kwannon. An unforgettable moment! The room was filled with a wonderful stillness, for the perfect circle before us expressed the stillness emanating from the master.

When Master Hayashi handed me the paper I thanked him and asked: 'How does one set about becoming a master?' Whereupon he replied with a quiet smile, 'Just by letting the master who is in us come out.' Just letting him come out! As if it were so simple.

It takes a long time to arrive at such simplicity, the way taught by the masters of the East. It is the way of practice as they mean it—practice understood as *exercitium ad integrum*.

In all practice understood as *exercitium* man learns to conquer himself. At first, of course, intense alertness, a firm untiring will and great perseverance are needed to repeat the same thing again and again until finally the skill is perfected. But practice in the real sense begins only when technique as such has been mastered, for only then can the aspirant perceive to what extent self pride and the desire to shine, as well as fear of failure, obstruct his path. The cardinal point of all practice is the acquisition and consolidation of the vital body-centre.

The most persistent obstacle is the clinging to the I which, by its self-will, again and again prevents the manifestation of the acquired skill. Only when the interference of the I has been eliminated can the perfect achievement emerge—but then as the fruit of inner maturity. The intellect is no longer needed, the will is silent, the heart is quiet, and happily and surely a man accomplishes his work without effort.

Then *he* no longer shoots at the target but 'it' shoots for him.

The masterpiece is produced by a supernatural strength from within which can act only when the 'little I' no longer pushes itself forward. A man who, in any field, has once experienced this inner power and has once learned to surrender himself to it, stands at the beginning of a way on which he is borne along by a new, free, dedicated life-feeling.

The practice of Hara is based on an insight into the region where Man's deeper possibilities and powers have their roots, and consequently where, in the practice of any art, the physical centre of gravity should be. In the strengthened Hara this centre of gravity will have become second nature.

The more technical training of Hara is based upon the following considerations: Every action relating to work or deed is controlled from that centre-point generally known as the I. This I is present in various ways in all our intentional actions.

43

1. The I sees the aim of an act objectively, it 'fixes' it. It determines it and clings to it. This presupposes that the I also clings to *itself*, that is, that it clings unwaveringly to the object desired. In short, that it remains concentrated only on its object.

2. By virtue of this concentration, this objective fixing, whereby man remains firmly conscious of the object in mind and, on the other hand, by keeping himself in constant relationship with it, the motive power for any action is changed into purposeful will. Only unflagging concentration while the I keeps its object and itself in view, produces that one-pointedness and perseverance of will and aim which is the pre-requisite for any advance in technique, that is, until the technique has become automatic. But the inward gain of automatization lies eventually in the hope and possibility of withdrawing—neutralizing—the 'fixing' I. Only where the I-power is no longer needed can success, as it were, blossom forth of itself. And, conversely, only where perfect technique in deed or work is possible without the participation of the I can man, in the midst of his action, become aware of Being working within him, so that the act itself becomes the gateway to enlightenment.

3. The centre of consciousness to which, on the one hand we owe the ability to focus something firmly, to fix it objectively and to pursue it purposefully, but which, on the other, debars us from the deeper powers of Being, is only one—the 'formal' side—of the I. It is confronted by another side which determines the content aspect of self and world-experience. To experience a thing as I is therefore, dual: Man, by identifying himself with this centre of consciousness, conceives his experiences 'objectively', while as a subject, determined by a certain relationship to the world, he experiences the world in terms of his private purposes.

Understood thus, the I is the source of actions and

reactions in which man is reflected in his personal relation to himself and the world. The I, in the sense of this 'personal' I, is not only the formal, ever-unchanging condition for all objective experience, but also its own 'material' centre of experience. Imprisoned in this I, man has ultimately only one aim in view—to preserve himself in this transient existence. When his subjective life is completely controlled by this I, man strives to maintain and to preserve himself *qua* himself and shows this by his continual desire for appreciation, for acknowledgment of his 'position', as well as by his continual anxiety and fear of depreciation, under-estimation or even annihilation. He feels himself always somehow threatened and in everything he does he seeks security, recognition and power, seeks to safeguard himself, to shine and to rule. All these manifestations spring from what may be called the 'little ego'.

Every action motivated by the little ego is permeated by the fear of failure for this would endanger the ego's position, if only by loss of prestige. What a big role plays the fear of blame! Anxiety, the desire to shine, the fear of being hurt haunt all 'I'—conditioned actions and experiences like ever active ghosts; because in all his experiences man seeks affirmation, security and self-contentment.

This material side of the I means that we can never be sure of maintaining a selfless attitude or performing a really disinterested service. As long as a task or an action depend exclusively on our capacity for outward, material constancy or on controlled will-power, and both are motivated and controlled solely by the I, all human activity rests on a weak, uncertain foundation. Firmer ground is found only where man is rooted elsewhere, that is, when in his self- and his world-consciousness he is anchored, in something different. Therefore when the prime purpose of action is the perfection of an external achievement, it is imperative to find a different inner centre of gravity. When a man possesses fully developed Hara he has the strength and precision to perform actions which otherwise he could never achieve even with the most perfect technique, the closest attention or the strongest will-power. 'Only what is done with Hara succeeds completely.' Just as life as a whole can be lived in full perfection only when a man is truly one with his primordial Centre, so every manifestation of it—whether in battle, in art or in love—'succeeds' only for him who has gained Hara.

Chapter 4

Hara in the
Japanese Language

Everything that Hara stands for in Japan is reflected in the language. Knowledge of what the word *Hara* means in itself and in connection with other things will give a profounder insight into its essential meaning.

Hara, as we already know, means literally BELLY. For the whole region of the belly the Japanese also has the words *fukubu* and *onaka*. *Onaka* means literally 'the honoured middle' and is the term for belly as used by children and by the common people. *Hara* as well as *fukubu* and *onaka*, means roughly speaking the whole region from the stomach to the lower abdomen. And, as with us, it is divided into stomach, in Japanese *i*, and what is 'below the navel'. 'Below the navel' is called *kikai* and this word plays a certain part in connection with *tanden*, by which the Japanese mean the spot about two inches below the navel. And *tanden* means the centre of gravity as such, which is cultivated in the developed Hara.

Hara by itself and in connection with other words, has a far wider meaning than the word belly has for us. Of course there are in Japanese many phrases and idioms which refer exclusively to the physiological aspect of the belly, for example: *Hara ga itai*—'the stomach aches', or *Hara ga haru*—'the stomach is distended' (from too much food).

47

Further parallels to our terminology which refer to the non-physical aspects of Hara show that the belly, particularly 'the big belly' refer not only to bodily satisfactions but also to mental and emotional contentment. A big-bellied, portly, comfortable looking figure suggests to the Japanese, as it does to us, the idea of a man who lacks nothing. For the Japanese, as for us, the big belly conveys a sense of a comfortable, quiet satisfaction with life. The Japanese has also the term *haratsuzumi* meaning 'belly-drum': the belly in its taut fullness waiting, as it were, to be beaten like a drum—as if it wanted to 'sound'. *Haratsuzumi wo utsu* means 'to beat the belly-drum', that is 'to lead a contented life'.

Another expression often used is *kofuku gekijō*—known to every student of the Chinese classics—which means literally 'to beat the belly and tread on the earth'. It recalls a way of life of the ancient Chinese people during the reigns of the sacred emperors Yao and Shun, the age of the 'contented people'. *Kofuku gekijō* is the exact expression of this contentment. At that time the people lived peacefully without troubling much about the State, or paying attention to any political 'ideal'. That was the whole point—that they lived as if the Emperor were unnecessary. The people were content and practised *Kofuku gekijō*, i.e. cheerfully they thumped their big comfortable bellies and trod the earth, standing on the same spot. (Is it not always a bad sign in any age when even the common people begin to talk big about virtue and love of the fatherland?) Less positive is the expression *Hara* (or *Shifuku*) *wo koyasu*, 'to fatten one's belly'. It implies ill-gotten gains, underhand dealings, or being open to bribery.

We have the expressions 'to laugh until one bursts' or to laugh so much that 'one splits one's sides'. Equivalents can be found in Japanese. *Hara wo kakaeru* (to hold one's sides), *Hara no kawa wo yoseru* (to fold the belly skin)—both phrases indicating immoderate laughter—and *hofuku zettō sumu*, to hold one's sides and fall over backwards.

All these are idiomatic expressions whose equivalents can be found in the language and daily life of Western peoples. But now for those which are quite different.

The Japanese speak of *Hara no aru* (*nai*) *hito*, 'the man with (or without) belly'; of the *Hara no dekeita* (*dekite inai*) *hito*, 'the man who has managed (not managed) his belly'. They speak of *Hara no ōkii* or *ōkina* (or *chiisai* or *chiisana*) *hito*, 'the man with the big (or the small) belly' and also of the *Hara no hiroi* or *semai hito*, 'the man with the broad (or narrow) belly'. None of these implies a visible physiological difference but a difference in character, a psychological disposition.

What then is the meaning of *Hara no aru hito?* The whole of this book is concerned with just that. Here we can give only the general translations without going into detail about their connection with the belly or their deeper spiritual meanings. For the moment we need only say this: Hara implies for the Japanese all that he considers essential to man's character and destiny. Hara is the centre of the human body—but the body, because it is a human body, is more than a merely biological-physiological entity. It is at the same time the centre in a spiritual sense or, to be more accurate, a nature-given spiritual sense. All expressions and idioms containing the word Hara refer to the character in its *totality*, to the basic quality of a man's nature, his whole disposition, and hence to those special mental traits on which it depends and through which it is expressed.

What then is *Hara no aru hito?* The answer comprising all meanings is: a man with 'Centre'. *Hara no nai hito* is accordingly a man who lacks centre. The man who lacks centre easily loses his balance. Conversely, he who has it is always balanced. The man with centre has something that is tranquil and all-embracing. He has a quality of breadth. Just this is meant by the term *Hara no aru hito*. And when this quality is to be especially emphasised the Japanese speaks of

Hara no hirio hito. This, as well as *Hara no aru hito,* refers to the large-minded man, one who is magnanimous and warm-hearted as distinct from the *Hara no nai hito* or *semai hito,* one who is narrow-minded and petty. So understood, *Hara no aru hito* (and its opposite) have reference to one's attitude towards people, but they refer also to reactions, to sudden, unforeseen happenings—the way in which a man notices them, reacts to them and judges them.

The man with centre has calm, unprejudiced judgment. He knows what is important, what unimportant. He meets reality serenely and with detachment keeping his sense of proportion. The *Hara no aru hito* faces life calmly, is tranquil, ready for anything. Not because he is thick-skinned or tough but because he has a certain inner attitude. The mark of it is an inner, elasticity which enables him to conduct himself with the utmost matter-of-factness and composure in any situation. Thus the phrase, *Hara no aru hito,* also means, 'the man who always knows what to do'. Nothing upsets him. If suddenly fire breaks out and people begin to shout in wild confusion the *Hara no aru hito* does the right thing immediately and quietly, he ascertains the direction of the wind, rescues what is most important, fetches water, and behaves unhesitatingly in the way the emergency demands. The *Hara no nai hito* is the opposite of all this.

The *Hara no nai hito* applies to the man·without calm judgment. He lacks the measure which should be second nature. Therefore he reacts haphazardly and subjectively, arbitrarily and capriciously. He cannot distinguish between important and unimportant, essential and unessential. His judgment is not based upon facts but on temporary conditions and rests on subjective foundations, such as moods, whims, 'nerves'. The *Hara no nai hito* is easily startled, is nervous, not because he is particularly sensitive but because he lacks that inner axis which would prevent his being thrown off centre and which would enable him to deal with situations realistically. He is either one-tracked and rigid, mentally or emotionally fixed, or else he has no composure at all. In an emergency he behaves either with blind obstinacy or quite erratically.

Hara is only in slight measure innate. It is above all the result of persistent self-training and discipline, in fact the fruit of responsible, individual development. That is what the Japanese means when he speaks of the *Hara no dekita hito*, the man who has accomplished or finished his belly, that is, himself: for he is mature. If this development does not take place we have the *Hara no dekita inai hito*, someone who has not developed, who has remained immature, who is too young in the psychological sense. The Japanese also say *Hara no dekita inai hito wa hito no ue ni tatsu koto ga dekinai*: the man who has not finished his belly cannot stand above others (is not fit for leadership). This does not depend on age alone. It is often said of a young man, *Wakai keredomo hara ga dekite iru*, 'although he is young he already has a finished belly'. Nevertheless *Hara no dekito hito* as a rule applies mainly to older people, if only because the fruit of psychological and spiritual practice needs time to ripen.

Only in connection with more mature man, the *Hara no dekita hito*, can one speak of the *Hara no ōkii hito*, the man with the big belly. Here the word *ōkii*, big, has its special accent only in connection with *Hara*. It means, as mentioned above, generous, magnanimous and warm-hearted without any implication of weakness or indulgence. In connection with the phrase *Hara no ōkii hito* there is also the saying *seidaku awase nomu*, literally, 'to swallow the pure together with the impure,' in the sense of 'accepting' even 'welcoming everything' and giving everything its due place. Saigo Takamori is always cited as one who exemplified this attitude. He was famous for never saying anything disparaging about another. He knew how to give the right place even to the basest of men and to learn something from him. For that reason he was able not only to endure personal ill-fortune but even to welcome it. He could profit by any experience. This attitude shows something specifically Japanese. The Japanese are not fond of making moral judgments, except in rare instances. But their characteristic attitude is to affirm life as it is, to accept it and give it its due in its uniqueness, instead of trying to compose it into rational and ethical systems. Such at least is the popular ideal, in the face of which pointless grumbling is considered weak, and narrow-minded judgment despicable. Many Japanese therefore repudiate the saying of Confucius which warns against association with evil people and also the old proverb *shu ni majireba, akaku naru*, 'if you touch red you become red yourself.' They consider this point of view unenlightened and paltry, and oppose it with the attitude of the *Hara no ōkii hito* meaning one who is not satisfied with trying to wipe out the ignoble but is at all times prepared to find the positive in everything.

The *Hara no chiisai hito*, the man with the little belly, is always also a *Hara no dekite inai hito*, one who has not finished his belly. He is in every respect a picture of immaturity. He is narrow in his relations with others, is easily irritated, shows himself unfavourably impressed first by this and then by that and so alienates people. On the other hand he loves flattery and likes to associate with those who agree with him. Moreover, the *Hara no chiisai hito* cannot deal with the dark aspects of life. He is a petty moralist who actually fears true purity. He has inferiority complexes and, as always with this type, superiority tendencies at the same time. The I-addicted who forever safeguards himself can never be a *Hara no aru hito* and, conversely, a real *Hara no aru hito* with his sturdy acceptance of whatever comes his way is always calm and relaxed no matter what happens to him personally.

Thus 'Hara' is something which puts the *whole* man in a specific condition (state), indeed one could say, that he is a *'whole man'* only because of Hara. Where, however, Hara is lacking man is not yet 'whole'. This idea is also very obvious in other popular sayings. If one says of an action that it is done 'with the belly' one means that it is not done by any separate function, not by any specialized organ but by the 'whole' of the person, even though he may make use of this or that particular organ. In this sense, for example, one speaks of *Hara-goe*—belly-voice—or of *Hara de kangaeru*, 'to think with the belly.'

Hara in the true sense has nothing to do with being corpulent, that is, with having a big physical belly. Thus people with no outward belly may have belly in the psycho-spiritual sense and vice versa. This might give the impression that there is no physiological connection at all. In fact such a connection does exist but it is not immediately evident in relation to physical size. A first hint of this psycho-physical connection is afforded by the reality of the abdominal voice. The abdominal voice really comes from the abdomen and a person speaking from the larynx, the nose or the chest is, indeed different from one speaking from the abdomen. Everyone is familiar with these differences, and knows too that the differences in his own voice denote changing moods and mental attitudes. Terror can rob one of one's voice completely. Pain, fear and even worry can cause the voice more or less to stick in the throat or at least make it sound strained. Anyone who has learnt to pay a little attention to it, can easily distinguish changes of mood and attitude by changes in the voice of a speaker. But this is not our direct concern here. The point is to be aware from the outset of the interrelation of inner attitude and 'belly' in the physical sense. The connotations of Hara are primarily psycho-spiritual but the inner aspect always has its outward counterpart. Thus, the Japanese distinguish in general the voice coming only from the mouth or from the heart, from the one coming from the belly, and are very sensitive to the psychological significance of these variations. The *Har-goe*, the voice coming from the belly, is valued as an expression of integrated wholeness and total presence. Genuine belly voices always have volume and depth. If a man utters profound truths from the larynx the Japanese do not trust him. They consider him insincere.

A master judges the pupil's level of maturity by the timbre of his voice and in general the Japanese pay close attention to voices. They will really trust only those whose voices come from the belly.

The expression *Hara de kangaeru* in regard to thought, like *Hara-goe* in regard to the voice, indicates the participation of the whole man. *Hara de kangaeru* is the opposite of *atama de kangaeru* or even *atama nosaki de kangaeru*, 'to think with the head' or even 'with the top of the head'. The Japanese says, tapping his forehead with his finger, '*Koko de kangzeru no wa ikemasen*,' 'One must not think just with this' and often adds, '*Hara de kangaenasai*'— 'please think with your belly'. By this he means, 'not so rationally, intellectually but deeper, please, as a whole man, from the essence of your being.' But all this, of course, presupposes one thing, one has to 'have Hara'. Thus there is the phrase: *Hara no nai hito wa, Hara de kangaeru koto ga dekinai*, a man without belly cannot do belly-thinking. This is by no means a tautology. Even a man without belly can occasionally think with his belly. What matters, however, is not an accidental, momentary capacity, but one which has become second nature. Interesting also in this connection is the Japanese term for plan, *fukuan*, literally 'belly-project'. The term implies that only what comes from the belly, 'stands', has the 'long view' or 'firm ground', as distinct from the uncertain haphazard notion or the merely intellectual consideration.

Thus it becomes more and more clear that the word Hara denotes something that gives the man possessing it special faculties, active as well as passive, i.e. receptive. Hara gives rise to experiences transcending the range of the five senses but which do not necessarily coincide with those arising from instinct or intuition. 'Hara' means that entire receptive and creative organ which fundamentally *is* the 'whole man'—able to prove himself as such. We have already seen how the Hara-practice lifts a man out of the prison of his little ego and frees him to live and act from his state of wholeness.

'Self-consciousness' anchored in Hara is consciousness of a self larger than the mere I and, therefore not necessarily affected where the little I is touched or hurt. It is, at the same time, wider and capable of doing more than the little I can achieve. In this connection we should mention an interesting concept which plays an important part in the Japanese world: *haragei*, literally 'belly art'.

Haragei is every activity made perfect through Hara. Thus it includes every form of art. Perfect art can flower only in one who has attained wholeness. And, in the concept *haragei* the Hara-consciousness of the Japanese reaches its peak. He who has mastered *haragei* has in a measure achieved 'that'. All the 'Ways', e.g. the Way of the Tea Ceremony the Way of Archery, the Way of Sitting, the Way of Swordsmanship, etc. are, in the ideal, and in their highest form *haragei*. But in daily life also all genuine relationships between people, whether fleeting or enduring are characterized by *haragei*. Take for example conversation. Genuine conversation should be conducted as it were from belly to belly not from mouth and head. Mouth and head should rightly be merely organs, not forces in themselves.

We will give a specific example of *haragei*. A man walks along a road. A few yards behind him another follows. The man in front senses, without turning round, 'that fellow behind me is up to something'. But he calmly walks on without turning round. The pursuer who is indeed planning to attack him feels, 'the man knows what I have in mind' and then he feels, 'he must be strong' and so says to himself, 'better not start anything'. In this case *haragei* is present in both. In the case of the one walking in front it means perception. At the same time it means a power of radiation strong enough to reach the other. In the case of the foot-pad *haragei* is also his capacity, or rather his general state which makes it possible for him to sense the strength of his intended victim who, in fact, has done nothing but continues to walk on calmly. It would be easy to speak here of 'presentiment' or 'intuition' and yet these terms would not correspond to the facts of the situation. It was not a matter of a presentiment but of an exact perception, not a sudden intuition but the proof of a reliable warning-sense.

Moreover, with *Haragei* there is a capacity both for reception and for action, as though the man were a highly sensitive receiving set as well as a powerful transmitter.

The to and fro of question and answer in Zen is also *Haragei*. Here the intellect and the five senses alone are not sufficient. And yet *Haragei* is nothing 'supernatural', except for those to whom the 'natural' means only what they can conceive by means of their five senses and the intellect. One could put it the other way round and say that *Haragei* is precisely the ability of 'Nature' to express itself completely —un-hindered by the limitations of the five senses and the intellect.

So it can be seen that, through the increase of Hara and its culmination in *haragei*, an all-round transformation of all man's faculties takes place. He perceives reality more sensitively, is able to take in perceptions in a different way, assimilates them and therefore reacts differently and, finally radiates something different. He affects other people differently, and through a different power. The three fundamental re-actions to life and the world—perception, assimilation and response—change in the direction of an expansion, deepening and intensifying of the whole personality. It becomes altogether wider, deeper and more powerful.

Hara in the Japanese Language

The example of the man who feels his enemy following him but remains undisturbed, and who, by the strength of this calm keeps the other in check, shows in a special way those spiritual qualities which the Japanese think of immediately when Hara is mentioned—unconditional calm, that is, calm not dependant on any outward circumstances, together with heightened sensitivity and receptivity combined with an increased readiness to meet surprise, and the capacity for taking lightning decisions which can come only from genuine absence of tension.

We too have a word which well expresses a Japanese term. We speak of a 'sedate' person. In Japanese *Hara ga suwatte iru (suwatte inai)*, means a person whose belly is sedate, 'it sits' ('does not sit'). The opposite is *Hara ga tatsu (Haradachi)*, which means 'a person whose belly rises', who flares up, gets angry, in the same way as we say that a sedate person is not easily roused. For the Japanese *Hara suwatte imasu*, that is the 'sedate belly' implies not only a corresponding imperturbability of the heart, an indestructible composure and a state of relaxation but implies also a swift and certain striking power. The imperturbability characterizing the sedate man implies the steadiness of a tranquil mind prepared for anything. He is able to react appropriately in any situation and nothing throws him off balance.

Sitting, which is both outwardly and inwardly correct is possible only with Hara. Thus, *Hara ga suwatte imasu*, the hara-seat, not only refers to the position and weight of the belly within the whole body but also suggests the whole mood of stable sitting. This stability implies at once an outward and an inward balance: it means that the inner centre is situated in the right place in the physical body, as well as the right placing of the centre of gravity within the body. Thus the Japanese can say: *Hara ga suwatte iru toki ni wa chūshin ga shita ni aru ga—*. 'When the belly is sedate the centre is situated below'. *Hara ga tatsu to ue e utsuru—*

57

Hara

'When the belly rises it shifts upwards,' which also means that the unsettled centre has shifted to the upper region, therefore the over-all posture is unsure, unstable.

Suwatte iru and also *tatsu* has an intransitive as well as a transitive meaning. Thus one says: *Hara wo sueru*, 'to set the belly' or else 'to let it sit', e.g. in the phrase *Hara wo suete shigoto ni kakaru*—'with sedate belly', that is to approach something with easy imperturbability. Thus it is always a matter of developing the right centre and making it permanent, reliable. To achieve this the belly must be exercised, must be trained (*Hara wo neru*). In this connection *Hara wo neru* was much talked about during the war. It was one of the main slogans in a time when all were called upon to give of their utmost. But in *every* way, including the way of every art, *Hara wo neru* is the indispensable preparatory and constant exercise. In this sense the *Hara no nereta hito*, 'the man with the trained belly' is always the aim, while the *Hara no nerete inai hito*, 'the man with the untrained belly' is synonymous with 'beginner', one who has not yet achieved a consciously trained and strengthened Hara.

It must be pointed out again that the expression *Harawo neru* translated simply as 'belly training' or development does not suggest to our minds the spiritual, all-round human significance which is its actual meaning. Nevertheless it is indeed also a bodily exercise, chiefly concerned with the lower abdomen. Further, *Hara si sueru* means literally 'to let something sit in the belly'. It means to bear, to endure something, to hold out, to swallow, to take into oneself, to put up with what is unpleasant. For the Japanese these expressions do not imply resignation. They contrast with wrong attitudes when one's gorge rises and when one flies off. In the right frame of mind if, for an instant, something shakes a man and he almost flares up he will automatically suppress it and he does, in fact, press it down into his loins by making his lower abdomen firm. (It will be shown later that this is something quite different from what is called repression). Certainly it has its limits, depending upon the degree of one's training. The Japanese would say *Ano hito no kotoba wa Hara ni suekaneta*—I could no longer keep his words in my belly (endure), and then my belly rose (*Hara ga tatsu*). The anger has risen, come to the surface and broken through, whereas before it was neither 'suppressed' nor 'repressed' but simply not allowed to develop. Or it may happen that one, deliberately puts 'oneself' into one's anger, rages, as it were, consciously. The Japanese call this *Hara wo tateru.*

The expression, *Hara wo tateru*, in this sense means 'wrath', particularly if something is deeply felt as an injustice. An especially instructive phrase is the combination of *Hara* with *mushi*, worms. We know the expression, 'something is eating me', which has a quite different meaning from 'it turns my stomach'. If one says, 'it is eating me', or 'it gnaws at my vitals', something deeper is implied. To localize this deeper sensation we Westerners would not place it in the lower abdomen for it is there in the bowels that we feel sudden fright. When we say 'it is eating me up' we mean rather a feeling localised in the pit of the stomach or in the chest. That the Japanese feels this 'eating' further down may be due to the fact that he reacts less than we do in his individual ego.

The Japanese says, *Hara no mushi ga osamaranai*, the worms find no peace, or *Harano mushi ga shōchi senu*, the worms will not say yes, i.e. they do not obey, in the sense that the person cannot control his feelings. This expression is used only in this negative form. *Osamaru* means actually 'to put in order', e.g. 'the state is in order'. The meaning of *osamaru* then also points to a 'total' interpretation of *Hara no mushi ga osamaru*. And thus *Hara no mushi* means the not-having-been-put-in-order of the whole man. *Hara no mushi* in connection with *osamaranai* means a disturbance which is felt as a gnawing discomfort endangering the vital centre. There is also an interesting third meaning of *Hara no mushi* in the sense of a disorder *foretelling* something. One speaks of the *mushi no shirase*, of the 'communication of the worms', in the sense of 'premonition', something of telepathy. For example, a friend dies and the day before one had felt somehow out of order—in this case the Japanese says: *mushi ga shiraseta or mushi no shirase ga atta*, 'the worms announced it'.

If 'the worms find no peace' (*Hara no mushi ga osamarani*), it may happen that the 'belly swells' and then a *Haraise*, a fit of rage, ensues, in which one blows up in some substituted action because one cannot reach the real cause of the rage. The *ise* in *Haraise* is the noun form of the verb *iyasu*, to heal, to cure. When standing alone it is used only in medical terminology. But in connection with Hara it means 'to abreact' and so, in this sense, 'to still the belly'. *Haraise* means to act in such a way as to quell anger even though expressing it may bring relief. For example, *Haraise ni mado so kowasu*, 'to smash the window in order to heal the belly', (to quell the anger). But such notion is typical of the man who lacks a trained belly. Therefore, *Hara no aru hito wa Haraise no koto wo shitari wa shinai*, 'a man with belly' does not act from *Haraise*.

Hara is the seat of good and bad intentions, the hidden place where one is 'up to something'. The Japanese say: *Kuchi wa warui keredomo Hara no naka ni wa nani mo nai*, 'although she has a bad mouth (a sharp tongue) she has nothing evil in the belly'. Perhaps an equivalent English expression would be 'His bark is worse than his bite'. On the other hand there is the phrase: *Hara ni ichimitsu aru hito*, meaning one who has something in the belly, one who is hiding something either just for the time being or because it is his nature to do so, one who is deceitful or untrustworthy. The word *ichimotsu* in this connection also has a special meaning, it means, 'the little from which great things may come'. *Kokan no ichimotsu*, 'the part between the legs', is a popular term for testicles. The opposite of *Hara no ichimotsu aru hito* is the man who *Hara no naka wo watte misemasu*, 'shows what is inside his belly by simply opening it,' which means he expresses himself frankly and sincerely, or *Hara no naka wo watte hanashiau*, 'talks while opening his abdomen'. In the same sense they say *Hara wo waru* or *Hara wo miseru* which means sincerity.

If one is uncertain about what a man is up to or whether he is up to anything and wants to find out his intentions one says, *Hara wo saguru*, 'to investigate his belly'. A man having no wrong intentions who is being investigated in this way may say itakunai *Hara wo sagureru*, 'a belly is being investigated which is not painful, that has nothing the matter with it, meaning that for no cause he is being treated with suspicion'. But only the *Hara no kirei na hito* has a right to protest, that is the man with a 'clean belly' who has no bad intentions whatsoever. The *Hara nokuroi (haraguroi) hito*, a bad man, one with a black belly full of evil intentions has no right to complain.

Finally, two more expressions which show the central significance of the belly, the first a proverb: *Seni Hara wa heerarenu*, 'one cannot exchange the belly for the back' in the sense of, 'one does not give something essential for something unessential'. And finally, the famous word *Harakiri Hara wo kiru* means to split the belly. For the Samurai the word is *seppuku*, for the commoner *Harakiri*. The fatal incision is made in the belly because for the Japanese it is the actual seat of life.

II
Hara in its General
Human Significance

Eastern and Western Views of Hara

(a) *The General Significance of the Centre of the Body*

In all that has been said until now Hara has appeared as a phenomenon of Japanese life only. But if Hara were nothing but an aspect of Eastern life it would be of merely ethnological interest and the purpose of studying it would be only to obtain a deeper understanding of Eastern people and their way of life. But the longer one studies Hara as understood by the Japanese the more obvious it becomes that the term expresses not just a specifically Japanese phenomenon but one that is universal and valid for all mankind. It is a prime factor of all human life, the realization and practise of which is of equal concern to ourselves.

The over-all human significance of Hara becomes evident in examples from Japanese life. It becomes a certainty as soon as one begins to practice it for oneself. From experiences gained through Hara one comes to see that it contains a hidden 'treasure of life' which is man's birthright, which was lost in the evolution of his consciousness, and which he must re-discover and practise as a prerequisite for all higher development.

Investigation of the over-all human significance of Hara is, for the European, overshadowed from the outset by the question of how closely the special importance given to the realization and practise of it in Japanese life is connected simply with the general Oriental character and outlook. A decision as to what importance Hara may have for us can of course be made only in relation to a Western scale of values. In exactly the same degree as the whole Western tradition and culture differs from that of the East the meaning and value of Hara will be different.

Because of the very nature of his mentality as well as because of his Christian tradition it seems to a European not only surprising but even odd that the discovery of the right bodily centre should be possible only by a downward shift of the centre of gravity. Is this really indispensable for Western man? A final answer to the question necessitates a deeper penetration into the phenomenon of Hara. For the moment let us say only this much:—

From the standpoint of the West, 'heart' and 'head'—the spheres of the individual soul and of the objective intellect respectively—play a completely different and more important role, not only in their secular but also in their spiritual connotation, than they do in the East where neither man's ego nor his intellectuality has ever been given the importance that they have for us. Similarly in the East 'mind' has never gained the significance it has for Western humanity, whether understood in the sense of 'ratio', or of 'objective mind' as embodied in our system of values and achievements, or of an intuitive perception of a transcendental system of 'inner images'.

But whatever may be the relation of the basic, vital centre, the 'earth' centre, to the higher centres one thing is certain—without awareness of it there can be no progressive opening of the Self to the meaning of the higher centres. (It must not be forgotten that the East also knows about the 'circulation of the Light' which indeed flows through the 'earth' centre but does not flow out or culminate there.) Where this meaning is sought in a transformation which ultimately lies in the spiritual sphere and is realized in the unfolding of the soul, there also the importance of that centre which shelters the great, primal Unity cannot be passed over. The realization of the truly spiritual Mind is possible only by a calling back of the limiting and always dualistic I-mind, that is, by merging it with the original Unity of life beyond all dichotomy. In every case where a Western man reached the highest development it was possible only because he had first traversed the 'deep dark'. The descent into the centre of the earth must always precede the ultimate ascent of the spirit.

(b) The European Attitude to the Belly

Everyone has a more or less conscious idea of how people ought to look and how he himself would like to look. He judges the figure of another accordingly, and, in his own case suffers from any disparity between his ideal and the figure he himself actually cuts. One's self-confidence is influenced more than is generally realized by an unconscious judgment of one's own appearance.

The ideal of the perfect figure, more or less conscious, differs according to character, age, outlook on life, cultural tradition and fashion. The ideal however is always determined by three factors—size, proportion and shape. Thus a figure may conflict with an inner ideal by being too full or too lean, or because the distribution of weight does not correspond to the 'right' proportions, or because it looks tight and confined, or, on the other hand, loose and 'uncontained'.

Despite individual differences, Western man today is generally afraid of being too stout; he seeks a harmony which has its centre of gravity in the upper part of the body, and he clearly prefers the confined to the too expansive. All this manifests itself in a universal rejection of the belly. Nothing is more opposed to the modern Western ideal of beauty than the big belly.

But, not content with rejecting the fat belly, we are prejudiced against any belly whatsoever. The ideal 'good figure'—not only in the case of women—is flat-bellied if not actually bellyless. For the young body this is justifiable, but even the perfectly natural increase of volume from a certain age onward is noted with regret, and the genial unconcern with which the landlord of the Golden Lion or the worthy vicar, the portly managing director or dear old Uncle George candidly acknowledge their abdominal centre of gravity is received with that indulgent smile generally conceded to people whose existence one willingly accepts but whom one would not wish to resemble in appearance.

The unpopularity of the belly is due to two converging factors. One is simply the unthinking acceptance of fashion, while the other is rooted in an intellectual notion. A big belly, or even a tendency to one, is regarded as a sort of mental fatty degeneration, a coarsening tantamount to a decline of all the mind's faculties. Secondly, it is equated with a loss of elasticity, particularly of mental energy; in fact, with increased materiality and cumbersomeness—things which modern man dislikes because he is always aiming at agility, at speed and the upward thrust. High-heeled shoes and padded shoulders stress these up-going tendencies. The urge to transcend gravity is quite natural to man as a spiritual being, but the desire to break loose from the vitalizing bond with the solid earth is in conflict with the law of his terrestial existence. Finally, many people regard the frank avowal of a prominent belly as an offence against 'good form'.

In view of these prejudices against the belly as such (which understandably reject the suggestion of excess in favour of an unnatural deficiency) it is instructive and perhaps surprising to observe how rarely European art, in the representation of the nude, shows evidence of such prejudices.

The changing representations of the human body in art reflect the changes in each period of man's outlook on life. In the classical art of antiquity we find the ideal of the unity of heaven and earth, and in different periods of European culture an alternation between the joyous-sensual affirmation of this world and the turning to the world of the spirit. But that the physical centre of gravity lying in the middle of the body should often lead to an emphasis on the belly—particularly in the representation of the female body—seems an instinctive thing arising naturally from a feeling for the beauty of the human form. The affirmation of this centre of gravity irrespective of the size of the body, is what matters. The present day rejection of the belly is unnatural and betokens a misguided way of thinking. It shows that the natural instinct for the true bodily centre of gravity has been lost.

But the natural affirmation of the belly which can still be found not only in art but also among the broad masses of the people does not necessarily imply any knowledge of Hara.

It is possible to speak of Hara in its full meaning solely in those cases where the natural centre not only works of itself but where it is consciously used to determine posture. An unconscious understanding of the value of the belly in no way denotes the possession of Hara. Hara means an understanding of the significance of the middle of the body as the foundation of an over-all feeling for life. Its full existence as we see it in the life of the Japanese and as, in our opinion, the European should develop it, has its precursor in the phenomenon of the 'natural Hara'. Here it is not yet realized in its full significance, let alone consolidated by conscious effort, but it has already risen above a blind, unthinking acceptance of the mere belly. A brief reference to the natural Hara as actually found in the West may help to remove any idea that an affirmation of Hara by Europeans is somehow un-Western and hence artificial.

Hara

(c) *Natural Hara*

The development of Hara depends on a basic factor of our ordinary human life, just like digestion, heart-beat, breathing or any other natural function by which we live. Understood thus it is beyond good and evil, as is our physical strength. And yet its existence, like the existence of natural vitality, is a necessary pre-condition for the development of the highest levels of life. Hara is the very embodiment of man's contact with the fundamental powers of the Greater Life manifested in him. It is a gift from life which is his without his having earned it. But only by preserving a right centre of gravity can it unfold its fullest meaning.

As the ego-consciousness develops, contact with primal, basic forces is usually lost and as long as a man relies mainly upon his ego he is obliged to replace the deeper forces by the use of his reason and will.

Nevertheless there are men who have not only never completely lost their original contact with Great Nature, but who are continually nourished by it both in their self-consciousness and their life-consciousness. A firm anchorage in the forces of original Nature acts like a plummet by means of which such a man will always automatically swing back into his right centre of gravity even though for a time he may fall out of it. Unconsciously he is guided by it even when his conscious life circles around other things.

Thus a man's conscious life may revolve around a beloved person, a task, a God-concept, even around his own ego, and yet, behind it, like a hidden spring from which his rational life also draws its energy, always reaching out for wholeness, this natural centre may be at work controlling and guiding him. In such a case, no matter what conditions him in his waking state he has at his disposal an elemental force which sustains, shapes and guides him, maintaining him in harmony whatever his life situations may be. Even dangers which threaten his security, his aims and his safety never completely shatter his faith and trust in life, because his basic vital centre has not been affected. What carries him through comes not from without nor is it based on his ego; it springs from a lasting contact with sustaining inner depths. In the man with natural Hara it can work un-hindered and in all spheres of life, for psycho-spiritual no less than the physical forces all have their inexhaustible source of strength and order within it.

This sustaining, ordering and healing strength rooted in the fundamental unity of life is veiled, however, as soon as a man, relying on his rational powers, falls into the delusion that he can do everything by and through himself. Therefore we usually find natural Hara where rational life-conscious-ness is not yet formed, as for instance in the healthy-minded child whose uninhibited self and life-consciousness do not rest upon his ability or his knowledge but are simply 'given'. We find natural Hara also in certain adults, even in those with very powerful ego drives. In such cases the connection with the primordial sources of life often brings disaster, because people with natural Hara have irresistible power over others.

The man whose ego is the controlling factor of his consciousness and who at the same time draws his energies from the forces of the basic, vital centre develops magical powers. Not only does he possess inexhaustible energy, often an unbelievable resistance to disease and even an apparent immunity to death, but he also makes others fall under his spell. He easily wins a blindly devoted following on whom he imprints his stamp and whom he unites and carries with him: unites, that is, round himself. Such a man, drawing power from the primordial sources of life, to which others have little or no access, and using them in the service of his ego, invariably brings disaster in his train. But not to stress the negative, destructive exemplars, it can be said that every born leader—whether in the sphere of politics, great enterprises or the spiritual life—draws his strength from the primordial forces of life.

Through his contact with these forces a man with such magical powers has an elemental contact with all those people whose collective dependence makes them defence-less against the elemental forces of life, i.e. those who are not yet, or are no longer in full possession of their normal judgment as individuals. The more a man grows away from his connection with the primal Unity of life, i.e. becomes intellectually differentiated and self-sufficient, the less susceptible he is to the influence of the 'magical' man. And yet, the more he is trapped in the blind alley of his ration-ality the readier he may become to open himself to the irrational. The tormenting emptiness of his up-rooted mind then makes him crave for a breath from the realms of a deeper life. This inner need not only opens him to the experience of Being but it can also make him susceptible to the occult in the bad sense, which includes black magic.

The magical powers of spiritual healers, great orators and dictators are incomprehensible unless one understands natural Hara. C. G. Carus quotes the observations of one of the men in Napoleon's train which directly bears this out and shows other characteristics of the working of Hara:

'The embonpoint of the Emperor is not a symptom of illness, on the contrary, it is a sign of strength. I was almost tempted to see something peculiar in the way in which the working of his mind and the knowledge of his strength reacted on his body. His face is in complete repose and yet there is an ease of movement in all his features. There is no restlessness, no grimacing. But his facial muscles instantly express every possible nuance of pleasure or displeasure.'

The ultimate fate of many of the great 'magicians' however, clearly shows that the strength drawn from Hara, though originally beyond good and evil, becomes destructive when incorporated with a self-seeking and presumptious ego. The more inflated it becomes the more the 'magician' loses his original secure relationship with the vital centre. If he loses the power and control coming from the deep he replaces it by the will to personal power and eventually the whole edifice collapses and destroys him with it.

There is another form of Hara, known to the ordinary man, which is not merely the expression of elemental strength but also an attribute of mature people who repose calmly in the fullness and vigour of their bodies, who are reliable and steadfast in their views and who radiate a kindly warmth. They obviously possess an imperturbable centre of gravity. Although found most often in older people with a certain degree of portliness, it has nothing in common with a paunch or a distended abdomen, or with exaggerated weight in the lower part of the body alone. The right weight shows rather in a firm fullness, an inner solidity and mature breadth. The 'man of good standing' and the 'sedate person' have their centre of gravity in the lower body. The supporting width of the trunk from the waist downwards is what often gives to old gentlemen and to matrons their essential dignity of bearing, the marks of the tranquil mind and of inner maturity. One finds this firm solidity down below in old craftsmen and master workmen whose long devotion to their craft and whose varied experience with people is, as it were, stored and preserved there.

A close observation of the whole manifestation shows that Hara means not the physical volume of the abdomen but rather the weight of an inner centre of gravity whose solidity frees its possessor from the unreliability of his ego-based forces. We recognise it in the attitude of all true kings and all truly religious people throughout the ages. It marks the appearance of the benevolent as well as the humble, expressing above all, freedom from conceit. This also throws light on the phenomenon of the 'Gothic belly'.

In the Romanesque and Gothic sculpture the belly is clearly stated and expresses strength, achieved self-renunciation and calm acceptance of the bond with earth. It shows the humility in which man, from the weakness of his I and from his bondage to the earth, opens himself to the Eternal. The Gothic belly seems to say: 'You cannot win heaven if you betray Earth.'

The classical reference in German literature to an unrecognised understanding of Hara occurs in Heinrich von Kleist's treatise *On the Puppet Theatre* from which we quote this passage:

'And what advantage would this puppet have over living dancers? What advantage? First of all a negative one, my dear friend, and that is that he would never put on airs. For putting on airs occurs, as you know, when the soul, the *vis motrix*, is located anywhere but in the centre of gravity of a given movement. Just observe P . . .' he continued, 'when she plays Daphne and, being pursued by Apollo, looks round at him. Her soul is in the small of her back; she bends as if she would break, like a Naiad from the school of Bernini. Or look at young F . . . when, as Paris, he stands among the three goddesses and awards the apple to Venus; his soul (it is almost frightening to watch) is in his elbow.' 'Such errors of judgment,' he added, breaking off, 'are unavoidable since we ate of the Tree of Knowledge. But Paradise is barred to us and the Angel stands behind us. We must travel round the world and see if, perchance, there is a back door left open to us anywhere.

'We see in the organic world how in proportion as thought is dim and weak, bodily grace becomes brighter and more dominant. Just as, at the intersection of two lines, a point on one side, after passing through infinity, suddenly appears on the other side; or the image in a concave mirror, after it has withdrawn into the infinite, suddenly appears close again, so also when knowledge has, as it were, passed through the Infinite grace re-appears. It appears most purely in that body-structure which has either unlimited consciousness or none at all—the god or the puppet.

'So then,' said I, somewhat lost, 'Do we have to eat of the Tree again in order to drop back into the state of innocence?' 'Assuredly,' he answered, 'that will be the last chapter in the history of the world.'

This is the last word on the subject. To find his right centre of gravity, which is Hara, man must eat for the second time from the Tree of Knowledge.

(*d*) *The Two Levels*
Consideration of the universal human value of Hara, like all questions concerning man, can be taken on two levels— on the level of the natural world-view, or on that of the supernatural or transcendental view.

Man must live in the world of space and time but, in it, he is intended to manifest the transcendental. In his Being his nature is transcendental, but he can fulfil this Being only if he lives in the (natural) world. Therefore man can be understood only in terms of the tension between his Being beyond space and time, and his life in space and time, whether his path leads to an intensification of the tension or to a resolving of it.

On his way to increasing consciousness man alienates himself from the original unity of life, relies on himself in action and in understanding, and develops out of his ego an outlook on life which we have called the natural world-view. This includes healthy, common-sense understanding, also scientific knowledge as long as it does not transcend the ordinary comprehension of the I. Only by transcending the comprehensible and by accepting the incomprehensible yet binding content of certain inner experiences can a man attain a new vision which surpasses as well as gives new meaning to the natural world-view.

Hara

To the extent that man entrenches himself in his natural world-view the Truth of Life is veiled. And yet the unity of the Divine, of which, in his Being he has a part, even though it is concealed by the pattern of his consciousness, still contains and embraces him. It works within him unceasingly, renewing and healing. Above all it puts him under an obligation to strive for increased individual consciousness which will no longer block his feeling of the Divine but will manifest it. From his earliest experience of consciousness in childhood and at every stage of his development, man is always animated at his deepest level by the need to re-discover the primal Unity. The meaning of everything he now understands and does from the standpoint of the natural world will be revealed to him ultimately only from the transcendental standpoint. What transcendence means for man will be revealed against the background of that rational world order in which he alienates himself from the transcendental. Thus every effort to recognize the reality of the human condition drives the seeker first to one pole, then to the other. There is no valid recognition of the reality, as anchored in the ego-mind, without some awareness of the reality of the Greater Life concealed in it and straining towards the light. But man has no access to the transcendental unless he has first clarified the structure of his own ego-centred consciousness. Yet all his thinking must necessarily start from his natural world-view. Therefore we will consider Hara first as a phenomenon of the natural world-view, and only later show, by implication, its transcendental significance.

III
Man with Hara

Chapter 1

The Living Form
Centred in Hara

The bodily appearance of man speaks to us of a triad.

(1) A particular relation to heaven and earth. Man cannot fly nor need he crawl. He is neither bird nor worm. He stands and moves upright, based on the earth but pointing towards heaven.

(2) A living contact with the world around him. He stands in a polar relationship to the world—on the one hand, separate from it on the other, bound to it in a living interchange.

(3) A particular relation to himself. At every stage of becoming he stands in a certain relationship to Life which constantly strives within him towards manifestation, unfoldment and oneness.

In his living outward form man revolves constantly round an inherent ideal image of a right relationship to heaven and earth, to the world and to himself. This image is always struggling for realization. But man's actual condition at any given moment corresponds only roughly to this image. When it corresponds to it fully then he is 'in order' which means:

Hara

(1) His physical appearance if right corresponds to his pre-destined position between heaven and earth. His upright posture shows that he is directed upwards and held downwards. It expresses clearly and harmoniously that man is both rooted in the earth and related to heaven, supported by the earth and at the same time striving heavenwards.

(2) If the living form corresponds to the correct relationship with the world, with humanity, with objects and with Nature, it indicates that he is closed as well as open to the world, clearly set off from it yet in contact with it, withheld and yet open. As a living form rightly oriented he breathes the world in, as it were, and breathes himself out into it.

(3) When the outward form shows man's right relationship with himself he appears both held and released, self-contained yet animated by a living dynamism, tensed and relaxed in a right alternation and balance.

A comparison of the bodily aspects expressing these relationships shows how and how much the man who has not yet found his vital centre, or who has lost it, violates the immanent laws of his outward form. Only where the tension of the whole is held in a true balance is it properly alive. Thus every offence against what he is meant to be appears as a disturbance of the balance between the two poles of his being.

(1) Thus we can see how people offend against the harmonious relationship between heaven and earth either by straining and stretching upwards or sagging downwards. In the latter case we get an impression of inertia or of downward pressure instead of that of a living support from the earth. What should be support then registers as an oppressive heaviness as though the figure were glued to the ground. Such a man does not walk he drags himself; he does not sit he slumps; he does not stand he just fails to collapse.

If the form errs in the opposite, the upward direction, the figure appears to strain upwards in a way that negates its vital relation to the earth. Such a man walks, stands or sits with his body hunched up. When walking he does not tread firmly but bobs up and down as if denying his natural weight. He does not straighten up naturally but twists up and thus very often he appears cramped, conceited or 'up in the air'.

In both these cases the right centre of gravity—the one connecting the upper and the lower—is lacking. When it is present the energies pointing to heaven and those affirming the earth meet in harmony. What is above is supported from below. What is below has a natural upward tendency. The figure grows upwards from below as the crown of a tree rises from a vertical trunk, deeply rooted. Thus the right posture expresses man's Yes to his bi-polar wholeness, his place between heaven and earth.

(2) Similarly lack of right relationship to the world is shown in the case of the man who does not admit the world, who shuts himself off from it or who, on the other hand, yields to it helplessly. In the first instance he appears not shut but shut out, his features like those of a clay figure are not alive but rigid, inert, showing no contact with anything. His reserve is not due to easy, natural detachment but to a rigid and guarded aloofness. The whole person gives the impression of being sustained by no living breath, of being lifeless. It does not vibrate in a vital interchange of I and You, does not breathe in a rhythm of inhalation and exhalation, of yielding and withholding, of admitting and flowing out. The capacity to open to the world is obviously lacking.

A totally different picture is present in the case where there is no reserve at all. The movements of such a person reveal a helpless abandon to the world which, as it were, threatens to swallow him. Nothing from within holds the figure together, there is no strength for detachment and resistance, it seems to dissolve and drift into its surroundings, and gives the impression of melting. A person of this kind moves as if he had no bones in his body, as if he had nothing holding him in one piece. There is no delineation and none of that detachment which is the sign of self-reliance and self-collectedness.

In both these cases the root centre producing the right state of the body is what is missing—that centre which makes possible a right independence and right contact between the self and the world. The relation to the world which man was destined for shows itself in a balanced tension between the two poles. Self and world must be able to function independently of each other and yet be related and connected. They must separate in order to find and unite with each other again, and become one in order that each may find itself. Thus right relationship to the world is shown only when the motions of yielding, of making contact and of admitting in no way suggest helpless self-surrender. The man at home in himself, that is the rightly centred man, lives in that undisturbed state where the eternal out and in of breathing goes on peacefully, in which he gives himself to the world without losing himself in it, abides there awhile without being swallowed by it, withdraws himself without thereby cutting himself off from it and remains alone without ever hardening himself.

(3) Man's right relationship to himself is lost where in the interplay of inner life and outer form a disparity appears, either as an excess of the driving force of life or as an exaggerated reserve and self-protection. There are people whose bodily aspect conveys the impression that their inner life is so overflowing that their inner form is quite lost. Such people seem shapeless, without inner order and direction. Their gestures are loose, unrestrained and not co-ordinated.

The Living Form Centred in Hara

In the opposite fault the living flow of movement is lacking. The gestures are inhibited and halting and in repose the figure appears folded in on itself. One feels no con-solidated core from which movement radiates outwards, and the whole figure seems to be bundled together by force of will, and perpetually in danger of breaking up and falling apart. Excessive rightness is then replaced by formlessness so it can be said that the indwelling life-force is stronger than its containing vessel, or, on the other hand, that the containing vessel, cramps the living core and crushes it like heavy armour. In both these cases what is lacking is the active centre which can either withhold or release and in which the conflict between outer form and inner life must ultimately be resolved.

When this centre functions rightly the whole impression is one of evident harmony with inner life. The inner and the outer exist not against but for each other. The visible form seems neither forced nor slack, neither dissolving nor rigid but just what it is, maintaining itself yet constantly adapting —in short alive. From moment to moment the inner life fulfils itself in a consistent outer form and conversely this form renews itself constantly from within. At every moment the outer appearance is the expression of a renewal of life, re-animating the whole again and again.

Always then the presence of the basic vital centre is expressed in the easy equilibrium of the two poles and if one preponderates over the other the result is a wrong relation to heaven and earth, to the world and to the self.

Just as failure to achieve the right centre always implies a disturbance of the living whole so the achievement of it demonstrates nothing less than that state in which the *whole* is kept alive in the right tension between the two poles.

When that centre is lacking a man falls from one extreme into the other. The hunched up type sooner or later collapses. The slack type every now and again rears up in exaggerated self-assertion. The man without centre either strongly rejects the world or weakly abandons himself to it and he who is in conflict with himself swings between inner disintegration and complete rigidity.

We have tried to show how the presence or the absence of the right bodily centre shows itself in man's whole outward appearance. In doing so it has become clear that the living form can be described only as the expression of an all-inclusive attitude (*Verfassung*). So the centre of gravity which can indeed be located in a definite region of the body represents nevertheless an inclination of the whole man, and which, although psychologically neutral, yet manifests itself in soul and body. This centre of gravity which reveals the overall inner attitude of man constitutes then the expression of a third element. What is this third element? Nothing less than the whole man—to be more exact, the man whose living wholeness manifests the perfect integration of his essential being and his life pattern.

Hara, understood as the right functioning of the vital centre, is the pre-requisite and proof of the life-form of an individual who, in his psycho-physical totality corresponds to the right relationship 'heaven and earth' to the world and to himself. Only if this has been fully grasped can one estimate what the achievement of Hara means in its widest sense and set about practising it in the right spirit as a manifestation of essential (*wesensgemässer Ganzheit*) oneness in the world.

Chapter 2

The Ego and the Vital Centre

The expression of the living human form whether true and correct or untrue and incorrect reveals the fact that in the 'right form' there exists an axis around which the bi-polar whole harmoniously revolves. The wrong form, lacking centre has no equilibrium and no clarity either in movement or posture. Where one of the poles predominates the vital centre is lacking.

Over-emphasis on one of the poles indicates either that the bodily centre of gravity has been shifted to the periphery (e.g. too far upwards) or the complete lack of any centre of gravity. The consequence in the former case is rigidity accumulating in the upper part of the body; and in the latter case a yielding to inner and outer forces which results in the dispersal of the whole form. It is in fact possible to show that, where no actual physical deformity exists all wrong forms can be traced to a single cause—to a mal-formed I. This may mean one of two things—that a man has either too much ego, that is, the ego is over-emphasized and the self is imprisoned in it, or that he has too little ego and is consequently defenceless and nakedly exposed to all the forces of life. When the expression of the human form carries conviction in its bearing and movement it betokens the existence of a correctly developed ego. But what is a correctly developed ego? In what way is it connected with the vital centre as betokened by Hara? What is the relationship between the ego and Hara?

The right growth of the I is a cardinal factor of human life. On it depends man's relation to the world, to himself and to the Transcendental. But as the study of psychology can yield valid results only if it is based on the metaphysical point of view so the problem of achieving a right ego, or of understanding the failure to achieve it, can be approached only from the standpoint of the Transcendental.

In the beginning and in the end, in the origin and in the unfolding of all life, stands the transcendental I AM. Behind, within and above all that exists man senses the Great I AM of all life as the 'stillness of Divine Being' from which all life proceeds and to which it returns. The Great I AM is the all embracing, divine spirit whose creative power lends forms to all beings and all things, and gives to man his consciousness. Every being is destined to live the I AM of the Divine in its own way, and man also in the way determined by his human nature. The 'lietmotiv' of man's life is determined by the different ways and degrees in which the Great I AM manifests—and veils—itself. When man attains the self-consciousness intended for him by Nature he not only says I am, but says, 'I am I'. The 'I' here meant is the centre of the natural human consciousness and the first prerequisite for a fully developed human life. It is the basis of self-consciousness and the central point of the world-consciousness of the natural man. As long as no firm 'I' exists a man is passively exposed to the forces of life and has not yet become an active individual. In infancy and also where primitive man still lives organically integrated in his community and in nature, there can be no question of genuine self-consciousness or of a world consciousness.

The 'I am I' denotes awareness of a firmly held identity in which three factors are asserted:

(1) The *stability* of the I throughout all changes.

The Ego and the Vital Centre

(2) The *uniqueness* of the I as distinct from everything else.

(3) The *demarcation* of the I vis-a-vis 'the other'.

Therefore in the consciousness of the man who says 'I' in this sense there is a splitting off from the primal Unity of Life which lies beyond the pairs of opposites. From the moment he says 'I am I' man experiences life through the opposites of subject and object, before and after, above and below, heaven and earth, mind and nature, etc. but above all he experiences the dichotomy between the I entrenched and latent within his consciousness pattern and his Being which strives unceasingly towards transformation and development.

In his essence every man in his individual way is part of the Great Being. His share in the unity and order of the Great Being is painfully concealed by the structure of his consciousness which is always based on the pairs of opposites. His consciousness pattern, centred in the ego and based on the opposites, not only marks a turning aside from the Greater Life but, just because of its tormenting narrowness can never still man's innate longing to return to the original Unity of Life. Yet without the right development of an ego there can be no fruitful *experience* of the transcendental Unity of Life. But to regain awareness of this unity is precisely man's *raison d'être*, the nerve centre of all human endeavour and the background of all his longing for happiness, fulfilment and peace.

The longing for release from suffering at the boundaries of the I-entrenched consciousness drives the man who wants to cross them to reflect upon the nature and structure of what is confining him, and to seek moreover a higher form of self-realization. This reflection is the first precondition for an intuitive perception of the way which will lead him out of his ego-shell towards an integration with the Great Being, as well as the way leading to a right re-orientation of his I in cases where its growth was injured in childhood.

87

Hara

The strength of the ego, its main concern and active principle is what may be called *fixing*. Man becomes I by thinking 'I am I', that is by establishing his identity with himself. In this way he takes his position, his stand. From this position the world is then seen as 'op-position' and so becomes a fixed 'object'. 'World' means a complex of things seen 'out there' as opposed to 'here' where one is oneself. Before that the world exists only as a complex web about us, as surroundings, not yet as a separate reality in itself. To find a firm stand in the ego and in an objectively established world is a necessity for man.

There are three things which belong to a well grown ego (1) the right stand, (2) the right form, and (3) the right limits. And as the component factors of living man must have necessarily not only a (1) static but also a dynamic significance, the right individual stand implies both the ability to swing back into the I-axis and to regain balance; (2) the right individual form, a preserving of the fundamental form throughout all changes; and (3) the right limits, the capacity for self-closing and self-opening. So the successful ego is (1), not a rigid point but the capacity for movement around a firm standing axis; and (2) a capacity for change without the loss of individual form; and (3) a penetrability which yet permits no breakdown of its boundaries.

With a well grown I the individual is confident of being equal to life. He also believes in an enduring sense, an established order of life in accordance with unvarying laws and values which he can deal with. And thirdly he feels in contact with the world which shelters him without extinguishing his individuality. Also with a well aspected I a man lives by values which are true and firm for him. He can deal with the never ending changeableness and transitoriness of life because his reactions are flexible. His adaptability comes from a deeper level not limited to his I. So his life because of its deeply mysterious flexibility swings around an axis which is firm. All this is lacking in the handicapped ego. In this case the axis as well as the I-shell are either too rigid or non-existent.

However the man with the correctly formed ego by no means lives solely from the strength of his I. It is true he lives as an I, but his existence springs from a level of being which reaches beyond it. Certainly the centre of his consciousness pattern is the ego, but a deeper, unconscious central force is also at work.

Through his dependence on the ego principle arises a two-fold danger. If the ego predominates too much the vital basic centre is suppressed because the static patterns of the ego bar access to the Great Being and the breath of the Greater Life. Or where no right ego has developed a man's consciousness pattern lacks the indispensable conditions for an integration with his being, and thus also for becoming aware of the form-giving and unifying basic centre. It is essential for an understanding of the significance of Hara to have an insight into the malformations of the I.

Chapter 3

Malformations of the I

The malformation which can be called the 'rigidified' I is due to too much autonomy in the I's function of fixing.

The man who is caught and held fast in his I clings stubbornly to what is already established and achieved and suffers from anything that involves change. Again and again he finds his stand in apparently secure 'positions' threatened. Although he suffers from life's opposition to his self-made ideas, he cannot defend himself except by entrenching himself ever more obstinately in his own point of view and acting according to his own 'system'. All his actions and transactions are conditioned by fixed ideas about what is or what ought to be, which, in his mind, should correspond to some comprehensible and indisputable ideal of perfection. He must always catalogue, classify, correct and try to make things better.

An itch for perfection is always a symptom of a too rigid I-shell. This ego-type is constantly irritated because the world does not fall in with his ideas about what ought to be. Poisoned or driven to desperation by the injustice and meaninglessness of life, he is sooner or later threatened by a nihilism which like a whirlpool destroys even his faith in God. 'What is the sense of it all?' Life is incompatible with the idea of an all-good, all-wise God and so he discards his former faith and stubbornly asserts the non-existence of God. That his faith was a pseudo-faith—because faith begins only where understanding ceases—the prisoner of the too-straitened I can never realize, nor that the sense of things is revealed only when he has foundered on the non-sense of his private, egocentric understandings and expectations.

In the conduct of practical daily life the I-prisoner shows an anxious striving for demonstrable security, and as he does not possess that fundamental trust in life which comes from an openness towards Being, he has no choice but to rely upon himself alone. His self-confidence rests solely upon what he knows, has and can do. So he is always concerned with improving and preserving his position, always in fear for his material security, in society very sensitive about his dignity, and when he feels himself attacked he stiffens or turns sour—becomes 'knotted up inside'. If the pressure of the world becomes greater than he can bear he is seized by fear.

In social relationships the I-prisoner is egoistic as well as egocentric. He finds it difficult to put himself in another's place because at bottom he is always revolving around himself. He cannot open and yield himself to another because, lacking a foothold in his being (Wesensgrund) he is always afraid of losing himself in such yielding. Dis-inclined to become one with others he never knows the sustaining force which a community can give. Because of the rigidity of his preconceived ideas he is not even in contact with himself. He cuts himself off from all that fullness and unifying strength in life which, deep within his being, wants to unfold and be at one with others. Thus by admitting only what does not upset his tenaciously held position he not only cuts himself off from the powers flowing towards him from the outside, but to the point of sterility, he is cut off from his own creative powers.

Integration with the wellsprings of Being is also denied him. He stagnates and cannot mature. And lastly no amount of success in the world can serve to satisfy his inner need. For every success which he attributes to his own efforts only strengthens and heightens the wall separating him from his own being. Here lies the explanation of the apparently incomprehensible fact that success in the world often brings no lasting blessings even to a 'good' person— indeed that fear, distrust and emptiness often increase in a successful man to exactly the same extent that he makes his way in the world, admired and envied by others.

Rigidity of the ego-shell is one of the malformations of the afflicted I; the opposite one is that of the I with no protective shell whatever. If in the former case the 'vessel of life' is too tight, in the latter no proper vessel has ever been formed. Such as it is it leaks everywhere. Its contours are indefinable and everything stands open. In this case the man lacks what is necessary not only for holding his own in the world but also for perceiving and realizing his own deeper nature—his being.

The man without ego boundaries cannot preserve his integrity against the world. He is exposed to it completely and has no support even against himself. He is helpless in the face of his own instincts and emotions. Yet in his complete dependence on his instincts and emotions he is nevertheless without constancy and direction.

Whereas the 'I-man' lives in an imaginary security and in the conviction of his own power, the man with insufficient I finds the forces of life arising over and over again as ever new problems. States of complete impotence when the world deals with him as it will alternate with aggressive or defensive attempts at self-preservation when he lashes out recklessly by way of compensation for his previous impotence. Furthermore he lacks the power to order and shape. He has disorder in him and around him and yet he suffers from the inability to organize his life and his world. He tends to adjust himself to such a degree that he loses himself. Therefore he is forced again and again to make compromises opposed to his nature. At times he escapes into generally accepted conventions and falls back on habits which he clings to pedantically, but which are really without inner life. He smarts under the pain of being misunderstood.

When he does give himself the man without an I never gives resolutely but lives uncomfortably in a state of fluid acquiescence. He loves and hates without restraint for he has nothing in himself to give him measure and balance. He lacks wise detachment. No wonder that such a man, ridden by a secret fear of being exposed, withdraws again and again into a cramped and protective aloofness just as, conversely, the I-man not only on occasion falls completely from his rigid form but even tries to break through his stony prison by means of some wild and liberating intoxication. The prisoner of the ego-shell is liable either to sudden explosive outbreaks or to equally sudden surrenders. The opposite type is liable to excesses of hardness and rigidity.

The deepest tragedy of the man with the under-developed I lies in his relation to the forces of the Great Life that are constantly striving within him towards realization. They break in on him and though often bringing him periods of deep bliss they cannot gain a permanent foothold in him. The blissful period passes leaving no trace because of his in- capacity to give it inner form. He plunges again and again from light into darkness, from joy into deep sorrow. All too defenceless and open, he is both overpowered from without and from within either by happiness or by grief but neither leaves any lasting trace. Happiness trickles away and un- happiness bears no fruit.

What the failures connected with the afflicted I really mean becomes clear if one realizes how they arise. The reason for them lies not so much in a man's innate character as in traumas experienced in early childhood. The healthy well cared-for child shows an innate confidence and sense of security in life. Innate here means ante-dating all experience, not conditioned by but pre-determining and influencing experience. The little child naturally expects the world to correspond to his feelings, and where the key figures of his infancy do not disappoint him his ego grows harmoniously into its right form. It 'succeeds' because he achieves its structure not in separation from the roots of his life, but in enduring contact with them. Out of this develops an attitude to life wherein the youth retains his natural self-confidence even when he fails or founders in the face of tasks and obstacles. Despite disappointments he retains his faith in the meaning and order of life and despite occasional isolation he still feels an immediate contact with his fellow-creatures, with God and with the world.

But when during his earliest years, the child's original, that is, the ontological feelings of confidence, trust and safety are betrayed by the failure of the key figures of his childhood he is thrown back on himself. This means that the connection between himself and his roots is henceforth twisted and that sure deep anchorage loosened which is the pre-requisite for a correctly developed ego—for no man ever stands solely in his ego. But if the original life connection has been lost and if the man relies solely on his ego he then receives his self-feeling as it were at 'second-hand'. Either it is based exclusively on the potential of his ego or on the other hand he achieves no sure self-feeling at all. In the first case there appears a person who tries, in more or less heroic defiance, to replace with his intellect and will what was lost in childhood and in the second one who simply gives up.

The opposite types of the afflicted ego as here briefly outlined are in reality infinitely more complex. The 'too much' as well as the 'too little' is hardly ever equally marked in all spheres of life but is divided into several partial ones. There is for example the man who in one respect has too much ego and in another too little. These mutually conflicting forms of the too much and the too little may vary according to constitution or to functional changes such as those caused by puberty, by the crises of middle life, the rigidity of old age, senility, or lastly by neurosis, and they can appear as partial ego and partial non-ego complexes which although mutually contradictory can yet exist side by side.

All the malformations of the ego express an inability to master the difficulties of life. Man experiences three primary difficulties—the danger and the transitoriness of life fill him with fear; its senselessness and injustice drive him to despair; its cruelty isolates him and plunges him into grief. Where in the midst of all these he still shows faith, trust and a feeling of being sheltered there may be a two-fold cause—it may be of an empirical nature based upon previous experiences of himself and his world. Or it may be of an 'a priori' nature, that is prior to all experience. It is the latter which reveals a contact with something other-worldly. If he has this a man holds his own in this world. If he does not have it his confidence, his faith and his sense of security rest on clay feet. Rootedness in a ground which cannot be shaken by any disturbing experience of the world is the meaning of Hara.

Chapter 4

Hara as Secular Power

From the beginning to the end of his life man is filled with anxiety about his standing in the world. He wants to maintain and to prove himself and therefore, strives for stability and security. He must be able both to make his way and to defend himself. If he has lost the connection with the Greater Life within himself or not yet regained it, he has to rely upon the faculties which he possesses in his I in order to master life. The man who has Hara builds not merely on the strength of his I, for he has already experienced two things: first, that the powers centred on and guided by his I as well as his personal self-feeling have their actual source elsewhere; secondly, that wherever he has entrenched himself within the narrow circle of his I, he becomes in fact weak and insecure. The influx of a deeper strength is blocked. One who has Hara, although using all the faculties of the I has learned when and how to withdraw his ego and to base himself on a different foundation from which his real strength, as well as his I strength, flows.

The man who has Hara at his disposal stands upright. He is not likely to lose his balance, either literally or figuratively, and if something happens which does upset him, or if circumstances temporarily force him to over-reach himself, he soon swings back into his vital centre.

One who has mastered the practice of Hara is also less

1 Horyuji-Kura, Boddhisattvis, from K. With, *Buddhistische Plastik in Japan*

2 Japanese tea ceremony

Below : The Kabuki Choir: from Werner Bischof, *Japan*, Manesse-Verlag, Conzett & Huber, Zurich

3 Horyuji-Kondo, Yumechigai-Kwannon
from K. With, *Buddhistische Plastik in Japan*

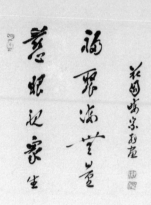

4 Master Kenran Umeji

Right : Master Ekyo Hayashi's painting of
Kwannon—the Goddess of Mercy (in
the possession of the author)

5 *left*: Mary Magdalene, from the Holy Sepulchre. Augustiner Museum, Freiburg

Right: The Synagogue. From *Der Bamberger Dom und seine Bildwerke*, by Walter Hege and Wilhelm Pinder, Deutscher Kunstverlag, Berlin

6 Yakushiji-Kodo, Nikko Bosatsu
from K. With, *Buddhistische Plastik in Japan*

Above: Young Zen monks in meditation. The Master sits in the chair

Left: The forebears of Christ, Chartres Cathedral. *Photo:* TEL Editeurs, Paris

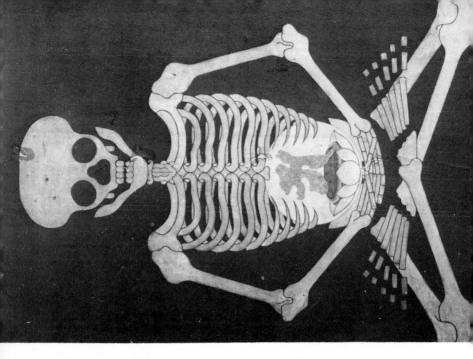

8 *Left*: The
Repentant Buddha,
at Gandhara, N.W.
India. Lahore
Museum, Pakistan

Right: Kakamona
Meditations
A-ji-Kan

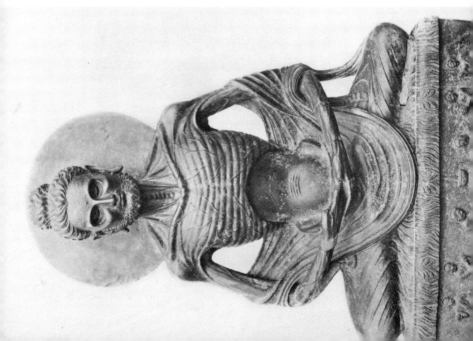

easily tired. By re-establishing the connection with his vital centre he always has access to reliable springs of new strength. He does not consume himself and he never spends himself completely. The more he learns to anchor himself in Hara the more he can shake off the disturbances of body and mind caused by the yoke of the I and clear the way for the powers regenerating him from the depths.

There is no sick person whose recovery is not blocked by inner cramp or tension. And no recovery that could not be hastened by loosening of tension. To exactly the extent that such tensions are connected with the fears of a troubled ego or the defiance of an obstinate one, they are released when a man has learned to drop his I and to surrender to that deeper strength which Hara surely opens to him. Hara thus means the capacity for physical renewal and 'stepping up'. It is always astonishing to see how much a person who has Hara can renew, increase and conserve his energy. One example can serve for many: Kenran Uneji, the archery master, bade his pupils test his arm muscles at the moment when his bow was drawn to its fullest extent—a bow which nobody but himself was able to draw. His muscles were completely relaxed. He laughed and said, 'Only beginners use muscle power—I draw simply with the spirit,' and he meant by that the power that comes from Hara.

Whenever a physical performance results from the right use of Hara that is, 'using one's middle', all the organs work as if in play, as functions of a whole, accurately and without straining. And, even in the smallest partial action, the great *whole* is at work. But the whole includes more than the powers comprehended and guided by the I. If the basic centre which releases the strength of the whole is missing, the limbs then have to be consciously directed by the will. The effect is unco-ordinated, without inner flow. There is fatigue and cramp soon follows. This is true of every action demanding physical strength, carrying, pushing, pulling, speaking, singing, writing, typing, dancing, climbing, cycling, etc. It is also true of every sport and every kind of work in house, field or workshop. Wherever work is done from Hara, that is, with a tranquil I and with the strength rising from the vital centre, the effort is reduced to a minimum because the movement occurs organically and is not executed by the I.

Hara also enables one to bear pain to an unusual degree. Indeed to the extent that a man has learned to drop his anxious safety-seeking I and to collect himself in his basic physical centre, he does not feel pain. It is as if the part that suffers physical pain were not present.

The I-imprisoned man diminishes the basic strength originally given to him by nature. There are many accounts of people in great danger who, by eliminating their I and meeting all resistance with Hara, passed through barriers which would have defeated them had they relied on themselves alone. It is as if there grew out of Hara a sphere of strength from which danger rebounds, before which obstacles yield and in which attacks find no lodgement. He who has no I-position to defend offers no target to the attacker and the enemy strikes thin air. Anyone resting securely in Hara is also immune against contagious diseases.

The man who has Hara can wait. He is patient in all situations and always has time. He can also look on calmly, feels no urge to interfere constantly. The more practised he is in Hara, and the more he has come to know this power which gives him tranquillity and patience, the more quickly he recognizes, in every stirring of impatience, that he has deviated from his own true centre and has fallen under the sway of his I.

The man who has Hara is composed. Thus Hara is salutary for every form of nervousness. Unnecessary movements cease and all restless jerking and twitching of the limbs. It is as if peace had entered the body, an inner calm which is not lifelessness but the expression of a tranquil, self-collected harmony.

Hara as Secular Power

People without Hara easily lose 'form'. They are quickly roused, irritable and lose face in untoward situations. Irritations either fail to touch people with Hara or they know how to deal with them.

Health and recovery from illness are also connected with a person's being in form. Just as cramp and tension obstruct recovery, so also does the lack of inner form. Even a merely ethical intention to maintain a right inner attitude towards illness is helpful, but control by will-power alone prevents the development of the inner form which corresponds to the deeper nature. When man has Hara he releases in every situation—including convalescence from illness—the unconscious creative forces of nature.

The bodily movements of the person with Hara are free and unforced; he sits, stands and moves with natural command. With his weight rightly placed. In the basic centre he is firm and stable, his limbs free from all rigidity and inhibition and so his own personal form emerges more clearly. From the right centre grows the right form both in repose and in movement; and that form is right which 'gives' naturally, which is instantly ready to change and adapt and yet always preserves its organic flow from within outwards.

Hara re-establishes man's unity with himself. In regard to his body this means that he is not in constant opposition to his elementary impulses which require freedom and action, nor is he obliged to be constantly deciding whether to affirm or to deny them. It is as if Hara opened within us a completely new region where our tangled energies can swing easily without necessarily discharging themselves in action. Many life-impulses which for one reason or another have to be suppressed, can, with Hara, be dismissed into a secret inner region whence they return as increased over-all strength. When this is understood Hara gives man a legitimate power over his sexuality. When the I with its imagination takes possession of a man and demands particular forms of fulfilment his sexuality creates an unbearable tension which has to be either repressed or lived out—alternatives often equally damaging. With Hara an inner door seems to open. Going through this door he lets fall his ego-based imagination-ridden idea of fulfilment, destructive tensions are resolved and the dammed-up forces acquire positive creative significance. To summarize: anchorage in the vital centre which is Hara guarantees man enjoyment of a power which enables him to master life in a new and different way. It is a *mysteriously sustaining*, ever *renewing*, *ordering* and *forming* power, as well as a *liberating* and *integrating* one.

As a spiritual being man seeks something beyond and above secure existence. He seeks completeness within himself and in the world. He is in search of an accomplished form which will perfectly actualize the inner meaning residing in it. Both in recognition and in action he is serving the 'objective', the idea latent in a thing, a work accomplished. He feels himself obligated by inherent laws and in addition he seeks his fellow man for what he is. He perceives him in his unique being.

Significant and effective accomplishment of any given objective is hindered by the pre-existence of firmly fixed ideas and concepts, and fixation within the ego results in an ineradicable entanglement within the sphere of the personal—all-too-personal.

Effective recognition, action and creation pre-supposes a detachment which will enable a man to perceive the 'other' in the other's own nature and at his own value. Only real detachment from an ego clinging to its position, and freedom from fixed pre-judgments makes possible an elasticity of functioning which is indispensable for the accomplishment of any objective undertaking.

All ability is blocked when a person is bound within his little I, when he faces his tasks with and from the wrong centre of gravity. For then he is either fixed or trapped. If he is able to free himself from the yoke of the ego and to place himself in the right centre he soon gains not only a correct perspective but he can also make the best use of his knowledge. Thus precision of functioning pre-supposes that flexibility-in-depth which is tantamount to the ego's ability to release its grip on the steering wheel to which it clings so tenaciously.

The highest kind of skill is shown in the long run by a 'letting-it-happen', which implies abandoning the already achieved, but it is blocked when each repetition calls for a conscious act of will. Such abandoning is synonymous with the letting go of the 'doing' I. When it no longer interferes, when ambition and self-seeking are absent and the necessary effort is unforced, skill and ability come into full play. For then a man allows his ability, freed of all personal factors, of all fixations, to be used as an instrument in the service of the deeper power which will do the work for him. For this power to take effect there must be an anchorage in Hara, where there is no ego.

Any clinging to the ego position is also a cause of intellectual poverty. It actually blinds a man to the new perspectives which open out at every step of advancing perception or understanding. It impedes the creative powers of the mind. But the man whose ego is continually held in check is constantly discovering new possibilities.

Hara liberates the creative imagination. One who is freed from the ego becomes aware of new images arising from deeper levels. This is proved by the inexhaustible wealth of imagery arising in dreams. The tissue of established concepts and images hampering the imagination becomes penetrable, whether in sleeping or in waking, only in the degree to which the ego withdraws and to which the individual in his waking state finds his centre of gravity elsewhere.

Thus in the mental realm, achieving Hara means the release of powers latent in the depths which endow man in all his activities with creative energy and a sense of actuality. Freed from the bondage of established patterns from the past, he is creatively united with the task in hand.

Chapter 5

Hara in Experience
Insight and Practice

Hara always has a two-fold meaning: possession of it gives one a special strength for living in this world. But this strength merely proves that one has gained contact with the other-worldly powers of one's being. Only through it is one enabled to realize consciously one's own being in the Great Being which is the ultimate meaning of life.

Man's integration with the Great Life and the evolution of his own true Self is the meaning of the *inner* way. To achieve Hara consciously means entering the inner way, and the strengthening of Hara means advance on the way. The mundane power which Hara bestows, seen from the inner way, is merely a by-product of the strengthened contact with the Greater Life. Supernatural power is released through man's liberation from the limitations of his ego. What that power is in itself cannot be explained. But it is possible to show the conditions on which it depends, how it appears as a force in the world, as well as in certain peculiar qualities of inner experience, and how it may be developed and put into practice in daily life. All progress on the inner way is dependent on three factors—experience, insight and practice.

Without experiences which render life unbearable and which make the hope of something new appear alluring and promising, there is no impulse towards inner change. But if painful life experience is not pondered and questioned, not raised to the level of insight, that impulse remains merely a feeling, a momentary desire. Only insight into what is necessary for real change can prove that that experience has been something more than a mirage. And if insight remains merely insight into the meaning of an experience (for man is always in danger of believing that he already is or can do what he has merely glimpsed as insight) still nothing will be changed. A new attitude has to be cultivated in order to ensure progress on a new path.

It is astonishing that the idea of training or practice as a decisive factor in personal development has disappeared so completely from the mind of modern man. Yet man can achieve nothing without practice. From his infant beginnings he has to learn what the animal knows by instinct; in childhood he has to be taught the practice of the first and most self-evident virtues. And all religions have constantly emphasized the necessity of practice. So it is hard to understand why people of our time should believe it possible to realize the Transcendental without '*exercitium*', spiritual practice. There can be no progress on the way to integration without practice in that state of mind which is its perpetual pre-condition. On the other hand practice without insight will be just as short-lived and sterile as insight without practice. Thus in regard to Hara we have to make clear the importance of experience, insight *and* practice. The decisive experiences for the realizing and strengthening of Hara are mainly those which one undergoes during the process of achieving it, that is, during the moments when one passes from the old to the new, from being without to being with Hara.

The most important insight along the path to Hara is the understanding both of the relation between ego and Being and of man's destiny—the manifestation of Being in the corrected life patterns of his 'I'. Furthermore insight is required into that whole condition of mind which obstructs the channel from ego to Being and from Being to ego, and understanding of what is necessary to free it. In consequence Hara practice has a two-fold aspect—

(1) an inward turning towards life and Being which is indispensable for right living, and

(2) the cultivation of a new attitude to life by which this inner-relatedness to Being can be fortified and proved. All that we have said of Hara so far has been concerned with insight. What now are the specific qualities of experience which present themselves in the achievement of Hara?

Chapter 6

The Strength, Breadth and Closeness Engendered by Hara

When awareness of Being arises in man his life-feeling undergoes a radical change. This awareness leads to the experience of definite qualities which have an unmistakable significance. Everything is permeated by a different light, attuned to a different key and brings a different taste. It is as if an invisible veil were lifted which had hitherto separated man from the world, from life and even from himself. All his experience and activity acquires a different character and a different valency.

It is no accident that the qualities revealed by the senses are frequently the first to indicate the new relation to life: since Being, is not apprehensible, and not to be fixed, conceptually they reveal the incomprehensible more easily than anything else.

All colours, for instance, as colours of conceptually fixed objects lose their immediacy and with it their original luminosity and transparence. But to one established in Hara sense-given qualities unfold their own depth. Again and again people who are beginning to experience Hara within themselves relate with amazement how, for example on a walk or a drive through the country, the intensity and depth of the colours depends on whether they are walking or sitting with or without Hara. Thus a man who had

recently begun to practice—this is one example out of
many—reported after a bus ride: 'I am sitting at the
window looking out on flowering meadows. Everything
passes quickly. I want to retain the pictures in my mind.
The thought arises, "In half an hour it will all be over, you
will get off the bus." The landscape outside immediately
becomes dull and devoid of meaning. The breath becomes
short, meets resistance below. The belly is pulled in,
tensed, the inner organs are drawn up and tight, without
life. As soon as I am aware of this I try to laugh, to let go,
to "drop it". I succeed, the belly comes alive again, the
intestines fall into place by their own weight, the abdominal
wall curves outward, breathing is once more easy and free,
a pleasant feeling rises from below. Everything is elastic,
nothing untoward can happen to me. And now everything
outside me is also changed; the same meadows are fresh
and as if newly created, the colours are full and brilliant,
the landscape is mysteriously alive. True, it passes almost
before I have seen it, but in each moment it is wholly
there. The thought of "afterwards" is compensated by the
fullness of the moment, I know that then too it will be
beautiful, just as it comes.'

Another example of changes in the colour-sense is to be
found in Aldous Huxley's treatise on Mescalin—a strange
and interesting treatise, though dangerous in its implications. Huxley relates his experience of the incredible
deepening of colour impressions during the Mescalin
intoxication. His explanation of it is perfectly correct, that
the fixing ego is dissolved by the action of the mescalin and
with it all those meanings which things bear only in
relation to the ego. In the shadow of pre-conceptions life
loses its original luminosity and so also does colour. The
experiment is interesting and instructive but it would be
dangerous to recommend it as a way of gaining access to
Being, for the experience here described is not legitimate.
The only experiences that are legitimate are those that

prove inner growth and result in personal development. All 'wonderful experiences' arising through intervention from without (e.g. through a drug), are illegitimate, for in such cases nothing remains but the memory of the intoxication.

It is certain that anyone making progress on the way will have experiences of a quite new kind and quality. He must take them seriously because they are road signs. Everything depends on recognizing and on taking seriously the signs which, as witnesses of Being, also denote progress on the way.

One of the special experiences connected with Hara is the sense of a new inner state of health which results from the downward shift of the bodily centre of gravity. The first thing one perceives is the freeing of the upper region, the I-region, as soon as one succeeds in letting oneself drop down to the lower body and, conversely, the feeling of tightness and stiffness as soon as the centre of gravity shifts upward again. And it is not only a physical liberation when the shoulders relax and the diaphragm becomes flexible and alive, when the lower body begins to support, relieve and free all that lies above it.

The presence of a Greater Life, noticed by one who is gaining Hara, is shown in the development of an entirely new life-feeling. And with the increase of Hara he will experience unfailingly sensations of a new *strength*, a new breadth and a new *nearness* and *warmth*.

The strength experienced is the strength of an inner firmness not created by us but given to us which cannot be explained by reason. It is in a miraculous way suddenly there. One needs only to yield to it trustfully and it bears one. It is a continual joy and surprise to learn from experience how the feeling of helplessness produced by some painful situation gives way, for no apparent reason, to a feeling of inner power, if one has only dared to free oneself from the grip of the frightened or angry ego and its defence-reactions of will, and instead, yields oneself trustfully to one's basic vital centre. The confidence which comes with the new strength cannot be explained rationally. But this precisely is the gift of Hara, that it opens man to the sustaining and protecting power of a Greater Life not to be comprehended logically.

It is as if a hitherto hidden spring had bubbled up within man giving him a vital strength and making him clear-sighted, forceful and shock proof. It enables him to accept every situation just as it is, to say Yes to it, neither approving it nor rejecting it. It enables him to accept quietly what the I would instantly and automatically thrust away, to accept anything and everything without asking why, and if necessary, to endure the unendurable. With this force a man can face danger fearlessly and meet it calmly. One who is really established in Hara can bear the threat of annihilation without falling a prey to weakening fear. It is as if he were in contact, indeed, as if he were at one with a Reality which nothing can threaten and which, even if *he* is bruised or broken, can be relied upon to restore him. No wonder that with this supernatural strength, which becomes more dependable the more he trusts it (but vanishes as soon as he mistrusts it)—no wonder he gains a new sureness in life and thus a new self-confidence.

Even more important than this new outward strength is the experience of the mysterious power itself. It is not a power one *has* but a power in which one *stands*. In it a man feels his share in a Reality to which he belongs more truly and is committed more deeply than he is to the 'world'. He senses that this power is something in which he as well as the world not only shares, but that out of it speaks his own life-ground (*Lebensgrund*) as well as that of the life-ground of the world (*Weltengrund*). But such insight, in its fullest depth and significance, comes only gradually in the course of long Hara-practice. One thing, however, he experiences at the outset: an expansion of his Self due to the experiences of this strength.

The Self he now knows is clearly no longer the old I but a wider, more comprehensive one. He becomes conscious of a new inner breadth, he feels an increase of inner volume as if he had burst the bonds confining him in his physical body. A strange feeling of boundlessness arises, a liberating breadth. He does not lose himself in it but, on the contrary, truly finds himself. A new breathing space, scope and sphere of action opens up and he realizes only then how confined he had been before, how imprisoned and isolated. The man without Hara has only a very small space within and around him.

The man who gains Hara enters into a new relation with the world which makes him both independent of it and yet connected with it in an unforced way. Uninhibited and without fear he can unite with it because he has found within himself a broader base of action. He can embrace the world and let himself be embraced by it because in his being he feels at one with it, and yet he can detach himself from it because his new Self, as distinct from his old I, is no longer bound down by it. The man without Hara is dependent on the world precisely because he lacks real connection with it; the man with Hara is constantly connected with it because he is independent of it.

For the prisoner of the I the world has no breadth. His whole consciousness at any given time is filled completely by what he sees at the moment or by whatever has taken possession of his feelings. When a man has found his basic centre the limited space-time realities take on a transcendental significance. His inner vision remains unlimited even when much assails him or when the particular intrudes on him and demands all the attention of his I. Because the man with Hara lives from a reality which cannot be pinned down he remains open in his relation to the world even when, at superficial levels of consciousness, his attention has to be sharply focused on something particular. And because all his feelings, conditioned by his world-experience, are embraced and permeated by an awareness of the other-worldly life and its order, they do not throw him off balance but are all transmuted into impulses which open him even more deeply to the Being which speaks from his deepest centre.

With Hara increasing a man joyously experiences a new closeness to himself and to the world, to people and things, to nature and God — a closeness beyond the opposites of near and far, cold and heat, sympathy and antipathy as felt by the I.

One can give explanations and causes for the feelings of strength, warmth and closeness—or their opposites—when they arise from the ego. His strength and his weakness can be explained by reason. But the forces arising from Being can never be explained for Being is the primordial ground of all things. What emanates from it is beyond the pairs of opposites into which all life is split when seen from the standpoint of the I. When the primordial Being fuses with the being of the individual he feels a support beyond any explainable worldly security, finds himself surrounded by a clarity beyond the reach of the world's sense and non-sense, and by a love transcending the world's loves and hates. The new breadth, is also beyond any contrasts of narrowness. Even in an environment oppressive for his I the man anchored in Hara experiences an immeasurable breadth of life in which a meaning is disclosed and where everything has its place even though his I can find neither sense nor comfort in it. The new Hara-given power lies beyond the opposites of strength and weakness which man feels only because of the inherent structure of his ego. So too the sense of closeness and warmth that he experiences are quite independent of the actual conditions of his life.

From the new centre a man feels a closeness to his fellow men that liberates him from loneliness even when, in his ego he is thrown back on himself and stands alone in the world. He feels neither accepted nor rejected by others, but sheltered and secure in life as a whole, and he radiates kindness quite indiscriminately. He stands anchored in the all-embracing unity of the ground of Being.

Thus Hara conveys to a man 'qualities' of transcendental significance. They are signs of his affinity to a life-reality both penetrating and surpassing all that is 'possessed, known and achieved', in fact everything that springs from the I's relation to the world. In Hara he participates in a deeper Being which fundamentally is his true nature but from which in his former condition, in the prison of his I, he was cut off. Through Hara he learns what essentially he *is*, as if he had now actually found the secret well-spring of his nature which formerly he knew only dimly and at odd moments. The emerging of his true original nature and with it of his new relation to Being now clears the way to his real Becoming.

Yet for all the importance of the signs showing the growth of Hara, it must be understood that the Being of which every man has a part at his deepest level is incorporated in Hara only as 'original Nature' and is real for him only at that level. It is still not real for him in any personal sense, let alone as 'Logos'. At first Hara opens the *earth centre*, only later comes the opening of the *heaven centre*. Man learns through Hara *what* he is as a living being. Later he learns *who* he is as an individual. He senses the law of primal Unity, but still does not know his individual structure. Through Hara he experiences the happiness and fruitfulness of something like a cosmic love, but not through it alone the love from person to person.

To everything that we have said so far about Hara—its capacity to give new strength, new understanding and the feeling of higher commitment—it should be added that all these are but fleeting gifts to anyone untrained in the practice of Hara. The reality that will renew a man's whole life and permanently transform him can be won only by long, faithful, and dedicated practice.

Chapter 7

The Order of Life in the Symbolism of the Body

If you ask anyone where in his body he feels his 'I' he will probably consider it a strange question at first, but pressed for an answer, he will reply either 'in the head' or 'in the chest' or he will indicate with a vague gesture the region of his stomach and heart. Only very rarely will anyone indicate a region further down. And this is understandable. Head, chest and heart, like everything above the navel, represent the spheres of the consciously thinking, willing and suffering I.

If a man localizes the position of his 'I' above the navel it is correct in so far as he has developed, as an ego, beyond the sphere of his unconscious life to the light of consciousness, since his general psychic level lies in the 'I-self'. The more he identifies himself with his I, however, and the more he bases himself within the sphere of its consciousness-pattern, the more he comes into conflict with everything excluded from it. This conflict will be the greater the more he allows the conscious to take precedence over the unconscious.

It is completely natural that a man should tend to give greater importance to the sphere he knows well and which he can control than to the one which he does not know at all and which moves him irrationally. It is also natural that he should put a higher value on the mind than on nature working within him, and should seek the Transcendental only above. It is natural because people nearly always view higher development as increasing consciousness in the purely rational or intellectual sense. But this idea leads into a blind alley because the only realities then perceived are those which the I can admit and comprehend. For the I-centred mind, with its moral values, the blind natural drives constitute a repellent and unworthy contradiction. The resulting conflict erects barriers against the natural life striving upward from the unconscious and obstructs the way to an all-round human development, more particularly the unfolding of *that* mind which transcends the overlordship of the purely rational. Instead of a hierarchic order based on the *Way* leading to the fully unfolded Self, a conflict arises in which the mainly rational man excludes and represses that part of his nature which he feels to be irrational, less valuable or even value-destructive. 'Above' and 'below' are then evaluated as high and low, noble and base, spiritual and material, light and dark.

Finally, such a man begins to see in unconscious Nature nothing but the threatening abyss, the downward pull. But in so seeing he not only cuts off and rules out the instinctive and emotional in the psychological sense, but also the sustaining, informing and liberating forces of Great Nature. To the extent that the tap root of his existence has disappeared from his awareness, he will, while striving for the 'crown of life', aspire misguidedly to heights existing only in his imagination. He becomes sapless and weak and gradually his life-stem dries out. By clinging to an impoverished and lifeless concept of values he blocks any integration with the underlying depths.

The tendency to depreciate and reject Nature is perhaps understandable at a certain level of development because the I naturally rejects whatever may threaten it. The man who at first knows the working of the unconscious only as the dark urges of instinct and desire, feels continually threatened in his well-ordered I by the power of his desiring nature. Whether it is a question of the repressed powers of his instincts or of the Greater Being prevented from unfolding, he feels himself driven by the unconscious, or threatened by explosions, and he likes to speak of the 'demon of the depths'. But what he calls 'demonic' is nothing other than the untamed vitality of the Whole, struggling towards consciousness, against that small part to which, in his limited 'I' he tries to reduce himself.

It is the suffering of man's heart which leads to the beginning of all actions. Whether or not such suffering is fruitful and leads him to self-fulfilment, that also he perceives in his heart. Around it is the chest expanding in exaltation or contracting in grief, then liver and stomach become involved—one speaks of 'butterflies', or a 'gnawing in the vitals'. In the centre of this middle region beats the heart which is uneasy and longs for peace. With the unrest of the heart all that is specifically human begins, and in its peace comes fulfilment. The unrest may be caused by the sorrows of this world, or it may also denote lack of the fulfilment of Being. But in the final analysis it always reveals man's separation from the divine Unity and his longing to merge himself with it anew.

The position of man between heaven and earth corresponds to the position of the soul between mind and nature, and this is represented in the symbolism of the body, by the position of the heart between head and abdomen. Heart, head and abdomen symbolize, even for the naïve man, soul, mind and nature, and represent three forms and three stages of consciousness. The dark, instinctive, sensual consciousness appears in utmost contrast to the light consciousness of the head. In between stands the intuitive-perceptive consciousness of the heart. And this triad, seen intellectually, consistutes not only a genetic, organic sequence but also a scale of values.

To begin with, man regards the instinctive consciousness merely as the opposite of the mind, for he knows as yet nothing of a development from the pre-personal, via the personal, to the supra-personal, wherein each stage pre-supposes and includes the preceding one. He sees, at first, only a succession of mutually exclusive forms of consciousness through which he ascends from his instinctive nature, through entanglement in personal feelings, to the height of rational thinking, clear and free from the shackles of instinctive as well as of emotional attachments. The development of the human being as a totality appears, from the viewpoint of the rational I as follows: first, the mastery of the instinctive drives, then overcoming the limitations of the subjective I and finally the ascent to the real 'objective' morally developed I. On this scheme his striving should result in his being the master of his instincts and the servant of his mind or spirit in the realm of his heart. But actually something quite different appears. Out of his heart's need it may one day dawn on him that the lost connection with the Ground of Being which he has regarded merely as Nature's dangerous dark work is ruining the wholeness of his life. In the same way he may realize that in orienting himself upwards by the sole strength of his mind, which lifts his conceptional thinking into a guiding principle, he is missing the truth of life. And one day the moment may come when the sufferer will perceive something beyond the boundaries of his shrunken understanding which opens up a new horizon. If he takes this experience seriously he will soon doubt the trustworthiness of his three-pronged scheme of development. The distinction of Below, Middle and Above in the sense that lower body, heart and head symbolize merely the instinct-bound, the worldly, and the rationally-fixed consciousness, will no longer satisfy him. For now it will be obvious that the way in which nature, soul and mind have been understood is merely the way in which the whole pattern of life has been reflected in the mirror of the I.

When the little I withdraws and its working pattern is no longer the sole guide to the recognition of reality, life will disclose different horizons, gain new dimensions, increase in breadth, height and depth. Those formulae in which man perceived his reality as threefold and arising from nature, will indeed recur as a pyramid of concepts, but then they will have a new meaning and a broader base. The region of the heart, as the medium of endurance and of self-proving in the world will still hold a central position. But like nature below and mind above the heart region itself will gain a wider significance. Nature, soul and mind will no longer be separate, self sufficient spheres but pointers to a supernatural whole. In the total experience of a wider life, instinctive nature, supporting the I from below, expands into Great Nature. The confined and suffering soul, enmeshed in its subjectivity, deepens into the Great Soul. And the mind, chained to the intellectually comprehensible, is lifted to the level of a Universal Consciousness.

In what sense does Nature in the new vision rise to Great Nature? It will enter into the inner life as the *operative unity of the Primordial* which a man will sense as his life-ground in whose undivided, pregnant unity all possibilities are contained.

What does the released mind find? It will continue to perceive life in images and patterns, but then every pattern, image and structure will take on a significance beyond all assertions and contradictions. It will then stand open to that Being which speaks intimately to man in symbols. Here the light of knowledge will be different in kind from that of conceptual thinking, where the fullness of being streams away in multiplicity, where the in-dwelling order of life is fixed in static patterns and where the primal unity of the Divine eludes the I-limited mind.

And what is meant by the deepening of the soul? Then, as before, the sphere of the soul will remain the specifically human element driven always by joy and sorrow and battling for fulfilment. But the meaning and origin of suffering will then be seen differently. A man will no longer suffer merely from the unfulfilled desires of his natural being, but from the lack of fulfilment of his true being which is part of the Greater Life. Indeed it is the Greater Life which will then suffer within him, for it is always striving with all its force to reveal itself in the love of man according to the laws of the awakened spirit.

So the effect of transcending the ego-centred pattern of life is threefold: as a clarification of the senses opening anew to the Primordial, as an illumination of the mind in the light of which the pattern of Being is disclosed, and as an awakening of the revealing function and nature of the heart.

When a man begins to feel again the original Unity of life, and in his widened consciousness, begins to know the true meaning of consciousness, he will realize to what extent the development for which he is destined is obstructed by the way his heart dwells within his fixing I, and his I within his unpurified heart. He will feel, perhaps only dimly, the necessity for a fundamentally different attitude demanding a new standpoint and a new start. As distinct from the rationalistic attitude of the I, in the new vision he will see the need for an ever renewed merging of himself with the undivided Unity. Compared with his hitherto accepted rule of holding fast to what he has already achieved and undertaking new things only within the framework of the old, this new challenge will constitute an extraordinary demand on him. And yet the renewal of his life depends on his complying with it.

To be able to fulfil his vocation, which is to prove and to bear witness to the Divine Being in his life, to ascend to the new mind, a man must first go down into the deeps of his whole and original nature. In order *to go out* to grasp the

fullness of the Primordial Unity he must first *go into* the
original emptiness. To be able to find his way to the true
light he must first plunge into the darkness of the untracked
Unity. Where these insights are glimpsed the necessity for
a fresh orientation will arise, and a new relationship to
nature, soul and mind. There must be a reversal of the
twisted, upward pull, imposed in good faith by the I, and
a swing back to the perception of the underlying reality
whence all life begins its way and its upward climb. The
way to Truth for the man held tight by his ego must be a
'backward turning'.

In the new vision the symbolism of the body also takes
on a different meaning. The head and the space above it
symbolize the mind and its realm as the totality of the
Divine order. The heart and its beating symbolize the soul
and its world—the realm where man testifies in love and
freedom to Being. The lower body symbolizes Nature
working in secret—the realm of the Divine Source. Here,
everything concerned with the Greater Life, is conceived,
carried and born. Here all renewal has its beginning and
from here alone it ascends. And here, therefore, everything
which the I regards as valid must be re-absorbed—idea,
image or concept— for all that contradicts the eternally
creative Being can be released only through transformation
and renewal. The consciousness-pattern of the I, the heart
stultified in the I, Nature confined within that I—all these
must be given up and left behind on the journey downwards
before man can begin his pilgrimage upward to the great
heights and the true light. First he must be reunited with
the earth which is his home. To achieve this is the real
purpose of the practice of Hara.

IV
Hara as Practice

Chapter 1

The Purpose and Pre-requisite of all Practice

In the centre of all practice serving the Inner Way stands the 'backward turning'. For this the ego caught on the ladder of its concepts and ideas, and struggling always to maintain its foothold, is not necessary. What is necessary is a movement which leads downwards to the all-dissolving, all-absorbing depth of the Source.

Even the ordinary man at the level of natural consciousness knows about the renewing strength of primordial Nature. Although the thinking and reflecting man, dominated by the intellect, seeks transcendence always and only 'above', unreflecting man has known since time immemorial, and still knows of a transcendence 'downwards'. A man who constructs a scale of values based only on his intellect puts Nature, understood as mere 'material', in the lowest rank. In his scale of values rational consciousness comes next and rising through the values of the true, the good and the beautiful, the peak is reached in the sacred. Nevertheless, from some inborn sense man knows that this order contains only half the truth. The analysing intellect knows, as the realm of Nature, only the values of the pleasant, the comfortable and the sensually desirable, all of which can be elevated only through 'sublimation'—by the efforts of the ego-will and consciousness.

But in a less intellectualized inner life something quite different appears. Anyone who has ever had the experience of finding himself, after the unbearable strain of life with all its duties and entanglements, once again among mountains and forests and running streams, and who feels the joyous affirmations of Nature released in himself knows very well that the glory he now tastes has nothing to do with any intellectually-imposed sublimations of his lower nature. It is a value in itself, bearing its own rapture and its own obligation. He senses the release of an in-dwelling life-force freeing him from the hampering rationalism of his life and healing him through a widening and deepening sense of being alive and a part of life. If it is then possible for a man to surrender himself wholly to the depth which breaks open in such an experience he is filled to overflowing with the numinous. It is as if, in the beneficent abundance and healing strength thus arising in him, he experienced Primordial Life itself as something divine, directly, quite apart from any consciousness of values such as truth, beauty and goodness. This shows that for the man living by his natural consciousness, there is already a sensual awareness of Transcendence out of which the divine Being speaks more directly than out of any intellectual structure of values or ideas. And as everyone knows, whatever it may be that releases the experience of Great Nature's abundance is the same which releases the heart trapped in its suffering and clears the mind to the brightness of its own light.

An understanding of the renewing powers of Primordial Life is revealed not only in that love of nature which is frequently the last refuge of the man lost in his ego-world, but has existed since time immemorial in the wisdom of myths and fairy-tales. No wonder then that a new discovery of man has also led in recent years to a new discovery of myths and fairy-tales. Here, in a thousand forms, recurs the theme of the descent into the depths which has to be endured. Without it there can be no right way to the heights. Knowledge of this downward journey into the dark realm of the earth, as a pre-requisite for deliverance from delusion and for a break-through of inner light, is the ultimate meaning not only of many fairy-tales but also of ancient rituals. The way of initiation, as taught by medieval alchemy, points to the same knowledge. It is mainly present day psychology which in response to modern man's suffering has revealed anew the significance of descending into the depths in order to reach the heights. To this field also belong the possibilities, as yet little recognized, which lie in work on breathing and posture. Too often they are belittled and considered by many merely as 'helpful methods'. Today the paramount problem is how, literally, 'to earth' people who are caught in the hypertrophy of the rational intellect. But if this 'earthing' consists merely in providing a temporary, good-for-the-health relaxation, or in releasing inhibited instinctive drives it becomes dangerous nonsense, for as such, it will simply lead from one blind alley into another.

Hara, as practice, means above all else right earthing.

Chapter 2

The Purpose and Limits of Practice

Only an understanding of the purpose and limits of practice will safeguard the aspirant from following wrong paths.

The more he opens himself to the way of practice the more important it is for him to realize clearly what he can in fact achieve through it. 'Whoe'er aspires unweariedly' may easily fall into the error of taking to himself the whole credit for any success he may have, especially as regular practice presupposes a tenacious will. This error can be avoided only if the aspirant continually remembers that the forces of nature, working without his knowledge and assistance, are always striving to heal and integrate him. No matter how deeply a man in his consciousness pattern may have estranged himself from Being, in his innermost self he will always have a share in its ever-unfolding and beneficent activity. Being works unsolicited in man and in all living creatures as the divine Life which strives ceaselessly to manifest itself in the perfection of its own creation. It is this vital urge within him that compels even the I-imprisoned man to strive for the blessings of Being. Thus, unknown to his conscious striving, Being is ever at work trying to break through man's shell and to enter the light of his consciousness. Fundamentally this urge of life towards the light is the primal force behind all human life and activity, but if the only channel it can find in a man runs through a hard ego-shell it will be choked and blocked. Yet the primal driving-force of the human will is basically co-determined, animated and winged by the striving of Being towards the light. Thus, even in practice carried on by personal will-power, the real motive-power of the seeking resides in what is sought. If then through practice a man begins to feel some contact with his Being, it is not an earned reward but a *gift* whose essence was already alive and at work in his endeavour. In other words, practice does not generate the experience of Being but only prepares the way for it. The grace which may flower from this experience is not the product of a doing but of a permitting of what fundamentally *is*, of what the aspirant himself *is* by reason of his participation in the Great Being within his own being. Practice therefore means ultimately just this: learning to let the in-dwelling reality of Being emerge.

Because that to which the aspirant methodically opens himself is at work without his help as a basic drive in all men, it can emerge also even in those who do not practice! The revelation of the divine Unity of Life does not depend simply on religious habits to reveal itself. Shocks and catastrophies can occur which pierce the armour of a man's I and these can bring sudden enlightenment. Indeed, if only the longing for it remains somewhere alive in him and the heart in its depth is ready, there can still be a hidden but progressive opening-up of the Divine Life without any deliberate practice. What man is capable of achieving by his own effort is very little compared to the quiet working of the Divine Being which unceasingly with a gentle force prompts him to open himself and pours into his life in countless ways unasked.

'What is the highest that man can achieve through practice?' I frequently asked Eastern masters. The reply was always, 'The readiness to let himself be seized'. However, a man is never released from the obligation to do his part in preparing for a break-through of the Divine. To the extent that he recognizes that he is on the wrong track and becomes aware of the attitudes and forces bedevilling and pushing him to self-destruction, he is bound to do everything in his power to find the right path. One means to this is by systematic practice. Practice is nothing but work towards illuminating that power which separates man from life. It means the adventure of opening himself without fear, of hearing and heeding all the signs through which Being speaks to him. At the beginning and end of all practice stands the re-rooting of the conscious life in that centre which epitomizes the original Oneness. To make this re-rooting possible to strengthen and establish it—all this is the meaning of 'Hara practice'.

The man who is either imprisoned in his ego or has not yet achieved one is suffering from the loss or non-existence of the right basic centre. True he strives in every way for inner oneness, but he seeks it from his I both in knowledge and in action, by means of intellectually-conceived systems, or alternatively he seeks it emotionally by a resolving of all contradictions. But in either case the wholeness of life will be missed because the split dividing it into subjective and objective still remains. The growth of consciousness which truly reveals the primal oneness is made impossible.

There is only one way out of this blind alley—to take the risk of leaping into that realm which the ego believes it has surmounted and which it fears. Only if a man dares to entrust himself again to the depth of his origin can he reach the height for which he was destined. In abandoning the consciousness anchored in his I and in relinquishing the world of opposites rooted in it, lies his sole chance for the unfolding of a higher form of consciousness which corresponds to the primal Oneness of Life. Only when the ego's form of consciousness is quickened by a higher law can it render man that service which is its real purpose. One way of winning this consciousness which is open to life itself is the practice of Hara. For Hara means nothing but that condition of man in which he is open to the primal Oneness of original life and which he can manifest *in his everyday living*. Hara is a connecting link between Being beyond space and time, and our existence in space and time. Hara is the germinating centre of that total state of mind in which man, liberated from the despotism of the I, becomes transparent to the creative and liberating influence of Primordial Life whose transcendental unity he shares in his own being.

Chapter 3

The Pre-requisites of all Practice

The practice of Hara, if it is to be successful, presupposes certain conditions and proceeds through certain stages. The conditions are:

(1) A *need*. A person must feel that his present form of life is unsatisfactory. Only when a real need is present can practice be seized on as a necessity and pursued effectively. Without need nothing new can come into being. This need results from the whole deep suffering of life caused by man's estrangement from the divine ground of Being. Neither the pain of failure in some particular life undertaking nor damage and loss in the field of worldly action is sufficient motive. Nor is that kind of interest sufficient which seeks new sensations (perhaps in the form of occult experiences), or some magical extension of the normal faculties, or recovery from poor health without too much effort.

(2) The second pre-requisite is an attitude in no sense related to the wish for increased outer efficiency but solely to the wish for inner growth, that is, progress on the inner way. The inner way is man's integration with his Being. The practice of Hara has meaning only as work towards and on this way. But as the aspirant must necessarily begin to practice in the light of his natural consciousness-patterns it is difficult for him to start rightly, as he is always inclined to

see the meaning and value of practice in the increase of his vitality and efficiency in the world. The fact, therefore, that practice does produce an increase in worldly efficiency further endangers the formation of a right attitude, and the beginner is therefore all too easily inclined to see the purpose of practice in these results. And so again he subordinates whatever he may have achieved to the service of his I which is and can be interested only in mastering life in this world. Such abuse of the supernatural, even 'magical' powers released through Hara can produce disastrous results. The I in its self-conceit, instead of being subdued or neutralized by practice, becomes further inflated. And it may happen one day that the forces illegitimately developed will turn against him who practises wrongly, exploding his still I-centred wholeness, and destroy him. Only to the extent that a man learns not to take himself as the measure of all things and the master of his life, but as a *subjectum dei*, as one submitting and owing obedient service to the Divine, will his practice be wholesome and right.

(3) The third, pre-requisite of all practice is a *strong will*. New things are always stimulating, but there can be no real inner growth without great perseverance. Practice as such is often easy but it is difficult to become a 'practiser'. Anyone not possessing great strength of character should not set out on the path of practice. He should indeed be warned against it, for the discontinuation of practice is disastrous to precisely the extent that it may have already helped a man to achieve some results. Anyone who has for a moment beheld a glimmer of the light, thanks to his practice, and has then abandoned it, will fall back into a greater darkness and for the rest of his life will never lose a feeling of guilt.

(4) Closely connected with the third is the fourth pre-requisite which is the capacity for total commitment. Only one who is able to subordinate his life as a whole to the obligation of practice will make progress. As long as

exercises are carried out only 'on the side', limited to certain hours or minutes, and as long as the whole day is not informed by them, nothing will be achieved. Also one who gives only a part of himself to practice—one who partially withholds—will accomplish nothing. The whole man is needed. What really matters is single-mindedness.

(5) The fifth pre-requisite is the capacity to keep silence. It is very natural that the beginner should want to speak of his practice and the new experiences gained through it. But in doing so he destroys everything and prevents the growth of the new man. In practice a new inner body grows secretly and it does not thrive on talk. The NEW which is developing can grow only in silence and draws strength from being dammed up. The only discussion which is permissible, which does not weaken, is that between master and pupil.

To sum up: the fundamental pre-requisites are: an inner need, right relation to the inner way, a persevering will, total participation and the capacity for keeping silence and, above all, a *turning to the Divine*. Only when practice is completely imbued with and supported by the aspirant's submission to the Divine will the door open to those experiences of Being which will permit further progress on the inner Way.

Chapter 4

Posture, Breath, Tension — as Starting Points of Practice

As the practice of Hara concerns the bringing forth of the transcendent unity of Primordial Life and with raising it to consciousness, the question arises as to where in man this oneness is manifested. The question is best answered by an observation familiar to anyone who has ever practised even for a short time sitting perfectly motionless. If he does it correctly he invariably notices after a while that it has a wholesome effect both on body and soul. Here a *third* factor clearly comes into evidence which is contained neither in the terms 'body' nor 'soul'. But what is this third? Nothing other than the whole man, that is, the sum total of those apparently separate functions in which the individual exists as a whole and which he never sees from the I-viewpoint. Of these functions there are three in particular: his individual posture, his way of breathing and the inter-relation of tension and relaxation prevailing within him. His general make-up or state therefore can be recognized and studied by the wrong working of any one of these functions and put right by practice until correct posture, correct breathing and the correct relation between tension and relaxation are all achieved. So the practice of Hara, understood as the whole content of a right life condition, can be approached from these three functions which are in themselves neutral.

It is surprising for the Westerner that training in posture, breathing and right tension should be of such far-reaching significance for the achievement of the right vital centre. It is bewildering for him because he sees these functions merely as bodily ones and therefore fails to understand how training them can give legitimate access to the Transcendental. This attitude, shown in the derogatory phrase often used about Yoga-practices, 'You can't realize God by breathing him in', is typical of the Western mind. Its naïvety shows the narrowness of the usual thought-pattern which regards the wholeness of man as split into the opposites of physical functions on the one hand and of psycho-spiritual functions on the other.

A more comprehensive thought-pattern cannot be achieved by the efforts (common enough nowadays under the general concept of psycho-somatics) to reconnect the two poles (body and soul) while still clinging to the idea of their separate reality. Rather it is necessary to explore paths which lead to the whole, *as a whole*. A good first step in this direction is the understanding that the unity of life is clearly expressed in all genuinely religious postures and gestures. In them one sees the individual in his entirety open and penetrable to the divine Being, so that all content and all states then become transparent. It is the reverent gesture or posture of the *whole* man that matters. But it is not only in specifically religious postures that the whole man can be seen. A similar wholeness is evident also in composed posture, right breathing and right relation between tension and relaxation. So it can be said that the starting point of training for the essential right human condition is by work on right posture, right breathing and right tension.

If then in the following pages we speak of the training of posture, breathing and the inter-action of tension and relaxation it is not—it must be emphatically pointed out—a matter of teaching any new exercises for posture, relaxation or breath control. It is much more an introduction to the exercise of such training to be understood as the means of progress on the inner way. Therefore we do not intend to add to the already existing arsenal of breathing and posture exercises any new methods for reaching old goals, but rather to point out what is necessary for placing posture, breathing and relaxation in the service of the inner way, never merely for the restoration or increase of efficiency and power in the outer life. We are concerned only with *practice in the service of man's inner vocation.*

Chapter 5

The Practice of Right Posture

What right posture with its centre of gravity in Hara means in the purely physical sense, can be easily demonstrated. A man standing in his ordinary posture will fall forward if he is suddenly pushed from behind. If he stands with Hara he feels surprisingly stable. Even a hard thrust cannot topple him over or even push him forward.

Right posture can be acquired only if one does three things: drop the shoulders, release the lower belly and put some degree of strength into it. For this it is sufficient to say 'I am, I feel myself down here, a little below the navel'. It would seem so easy to follow these instructions, but not only is it far more difficult than we suppose to effect a change in the bodily centre of gravity but long, long practice is needed before it becomes habitual. Indeed to learn to feel *oneself* constantly down there is tantamount to overcoming the unconscious dominance of the I, and to feeling oneself permanently rooted in a much deeper region. This new placing of the whole centre of gravity comes to full fruition only after years of practice. Yet, as with all spiritual exercises, everything is contained in the very first lesson. But the beginner cannot realize this.

The mistakes commonly made in this first practice are the following: the shoulders are not just allowed to drop but are pressed down. The belly is not simply released, it is thrust out. Distending it is not what is meant. If done in the right way the pit of the stomach falls in while the abdomen comes slightly forward. In this way the third mistake is avoided, the most usual and most easily concealed one, namely the mistake of tensing the region of the stomach while tensing the abdomen. What matters is that everything above the navel should be relaxed.

Further, the right practice of Hara requires first of all the discovery of a new support for holding the body upright. The aspirant must find this support in the lower part of the trunk. Until he does so he is either tense, wrenching himself upwards in order to stand, or slack, sagging down completely if he does not forcibly hold himself up. Support from the lower trunk, although most clearly felt in the belly, lies actually in the whole trunk. So the whole trunk will gain in firmness as soon as the belly is free and able to take weight from above, while the small of the back in particular will acquire a new vitality.

The achievement of right posture is soon noticed by certain signs. If a man has found his proper centre of gravity he soon feels, to his own surprise, not merely a physical freedom in the whole upper region of his body but also that his whole personality is different. His knees which in the old, hunched-up posture were stiff and pressed back have become supple and his whole person is less rigid. The firmness of the trunk gives a lift to the spinal column as though it were being pushed from below upwards. When holding himself erect in the wrong way a man forcibly thrusts his shoulders back, pushes his chest out and draws in both his belly and the small of his back, with the result that his vital middle region is constricted and diminished.

At the same time the neck becomes rigid, bull-necked indeed, while the head is bent back and the chin thrust out. This leads to cramp. But with Hara the uprightness of the body is no longer the result of will-power but comes by itself. The whole body finds itself in flexible equilibrium. The difference in the tension of the neck is a special criterion of right posture. It is as if a secret power soared up lightly from below and culminated in the free carriage of the head. And so the letting-go above gives concentration of strength below and the resulting easy freedom of the head has its counterpart in the sustaining weight of the trunk.

Thus the practice of Hara consists from the beginning in a constantly repeated letting-go or dropping down movement. Then one notices how from the vital middle region strength rises straight upward through the back and produces the sensation of being uplifted.

Actually it is difficult for most people to give up a certain top-heaviness connected with wrong posture. Even if for a moment an aspirant is able to shift his physical centre of gravity downwards, the next moment it shoots up again. And while he is gradually learning to hold Hara for longer periods he loses it again as soon as he is seriously occupied with something else until, after a long time, he has finally incorporated it as a permanent part of himself. Only to the extent that he carries out the exercise not merely in the physical sense, by dropping his shoulders, but also by dropping his persistent, clinging I, will he be able to achieve permanence in the new posture. Then indeed the inner transformation has begun. The 'new' is not merely a hitherto unknown physical support in the form of a fine strong spinal column but a new backbone to his whole feeling of life.

Anyone setting out to practice Hara naturally begins by straightening up his body into place. This is the first and lowest step. As soon as he experiences and realizes that this new intentionally adopted posture gives him a different feeling of life and that it brings with it a new inner attitude, he can, and indeed must, begin his work with this new inner attitude. He must not only stand differently, but stand as a different person for indeed the man who stays calmly in his body-centre *is* different from the one who either forcibly draws himself upwards or weakly sags downwards.

However, the practice of right sitting, standing or walking fulfils its real purpose only at the third stage. When the aspirant realizes that with increasing Hara-force he has become different from what he was before, he may suddenly realize that the power flowing into him from below is not the product of his will but comes from somewhere else, and that he has only to let it in and to guard it. It is this experience and the realization of its significance that raises the exercise to the third stage, when the aspirant by means of his reverent and upright posture becomes aware of Great Nature within him. He then realizes that his previous posture was not only blocking the forces now flowing into him from hitherto obstructed depths, but also that by his wrong posture he was violating a higher law, a law which he should express even in his outward appearance. So he tries to obey this law. The significance of this stage of realization and practice is fully clear only when both become fused with his everyday life. From then onward it is a continual source of wonder how this sinking into and yielding to his deepest level of being results all at once in a transformation and deepening of the meaning-content of every situation, in life as well as in the possibility of his mastering it, and how everything thus acquires a new perspective. It is only in this perspective that the full implications of Hara practice become visible and fruitful.

Chapter 6

Sitting with Hara

What is meant by 'sitting' with Hara and how it must be practised is best understood by those who can ride. One rides with Hara. Only with Hara does that flexible and yet firm, relaxed posture which keeps the rider balanced, and which gives him that unforced control over his horse, release that 'action in non-action' to which the horse willingly submits. The good rider sits erect but without tension, in form but without rigidity. Rider and horse form a unity—a unity of symbolic significance. The horse adapts itself to the rider because the rider has adapted himself to the horse. They feel each other, as it were, from centre to centre. And whatever the rider demands is achieved not by his conscious will but by the force of Hara which produces it, as it were, involuntarily.

Hara in sitting then means, as in standing or walking, a power of inner directedness brought about only because and in so far as all self-will has been eliminated and which permits the appearance of an outer form that is not made but has grown organically from within.

Right sitting in Hara is best understood by comparing it with wrong sitting. Very few people of our time still know how to sit correctly. It seems quite natural to us that a person when unoccupied should lounge and feel uncomfortable if he cannot lean back in his chair. But equally when occupied with sedentary work most people tend either to slackness on the one hand or rigidity and wrong tension on the other. So, in activity or in inactivity alike, they lose the benefit which correct sitting could bring. This benefit could be theirs if their lives were lived, consciously or unconsciously, from the strength lying in the vital centre.

Training in correct sitting should begin in childhood. But our educators are helpless in the face of the bad posture habits of children. The only thing teachers can do is to give the command 'sit up straight'. This produces nothing but a momentary rigid straightening up soon followed by a relapse into the old posture. It is impossible to calculate how much lasting damage is caused by the too tense or too slovenly postures in which children do their work at desks or tables, or what opportunities for character forming are missed merely because children do not learn to carry themselves in the right way. But how can they learn as long as the educators themselves in their ignorance pay no attention to the matter? Proper education and training ought to begin in early childhood. Children straighten their spines naturally and adults should not be too quick in urging them to do so. Particularly the natural straightening up from the small of the back which babies and children do involuntarily should not be interfered with by premature admonitions and help. The ability to bear himself upright from his own strength is one of those essential early experiences of childhood which are decisive for the foundation and development of a proper self-assurance in later life.

In right sitting as well as in right standing the shoulders are relaxed. Only in the released belly is that slight tension preserved which gives strength to the whole trunk. In the Hara-seat the aspirant feels the centre which keeps him in form, perhaps even more clearly than while standing. He is not rigidly anchored in it but swings constantly and lightly around it. Even when a person of sedentary occupation has to bend forward in outward activity he still remains in touch with his vital centre if he has Hara. The inner and the outer maintain their coherence.

The practice of right sitting is not necessarily confined to certain fixed times and conditions nor is it, as some believe, only possible cross-legged in the Buddha posture. Only one thing is important, the knees should not be higher than the hip-bones. With raised knees it is impossible for strength from the vital centre to flow in.

In right sitting, standing and walking Hara proves the threefold strength of the life-giving centre. First, it carries, forms and releases not only the body but the man himself as a whole. Second, it supports and gives him his inherent form. Third, it sets him free. The foundation which man gains through Hara is therefore not only of a physical nature but also of a psychological nature which can help him to overcome the malformations of the ego. By his posture when sitting the man without Hara gives evidence of a handicapped I. One of the surest signs of imprisonment in the I is the slightly raised shoulder. It is the expression of the suspicious I safeguarding itself. In this posture a man allows nothing to come close to him for fear that it may hurt him. He is not composed and never open to what comes his way. Let him root himself in Hara and the ego-tension will be dissolved, and with no over-susceptibility he will be receptive to whatever may come his way.

Practice of the sitting-posture should not be limited to certain hours but should be maintained whenever the aspirant sits down. The exercise of sitting is the most funda-mental of all. Here the practice of stillness has its source. A thousand secrets are hidden in simply sitting still. A person who has once learned to collect himself completely in his sitting will never again let a day pass without practising for at least half an hour for it is this which gives complete inner renewal, especially when he has learned to concentrate exclusively on the sitting, emptied of all thoughts and images. When the aspirant has fulfilled the basic condition

Sitting with Hara

of all work—to be turned with all his mind towards the
Highest—sitting in stillness will one day lead to his
becoming one with Being.

In the legend 'Of the Good Morning', the pauper asks
Master Eckhart, 'Who made thee holy, Brother?' and the
Master answers, 'Sitting still and my lofty thoughts and my
union with God.' And it is said of Master Dōgen (the
founder of the Sōtō sect of Zen whose sole exercise consists
in sitting), that when asked his opinion of the method
practised in the Rinzai sect, he answered, 'Very good,
very good'. 'How so?' the other asked. 'They practice the
Kōan don't they?' (the solving of an insoluble riddle).
'Well,' said Master Dōgen, 'there may be people who can
sit still only if they have something to think about. However
if they achieve enlightenment that way it is not thanks to
their thinking but to their sitting still.'

The practice of sitting as an exercise on the way demands
not only the right centre of gravity, but at the same time
the right 'tension-relaxation', and above all right breathing.

Chapter 7

Tension-Relaxation

For the development of the vital centre it is essential to have the right inter-action of tension and relaxation.

Modern man very rarely presents a picture of a harmonious whole held in a vital alternation between tension and relaxation. He lives in a constant alternation between hypertension and complete slackness. Even the relaxation exercises frequently practised nowadays seldom alter this. The 'autogenic'-training of J. H. Schultz, for example, is often misused, certainly against the intentions of its founder, in such a way that a person suffering from excessive tension seeks in these exercises merely a pleasant, melting sensation of complete relaxation. The actual release he finds is used and enjoyed only as compensation for his wrong tension. But inwardly it does no good at all and such practices fall into the arsenal of those methods whose fabrication and misuse are so characteristic of our welfare civilization, for they do nothing but enable people to live with impunity in their wrong attitudes and to evade the one thing that is needed: the finding of a different inner attitude (*Verfassung*).

When it comes to the inner way, the practice of relaxation has a completely different significance. It aims at man's liberation from the yoke of the I, leads him towards a progressively deepening awareness of the original Oneness of life and serves to strengthen that inner state which permits the Greater Life to manifest itself in our little lives. The practice of right tension and relaxation, no matter what techniques may be employed, is of value for the inner way only if the aspirant is not merely seeking physical comfort or the increase of his I-powers but wants to find that mysterious source of strength for its own sake.

Thus it becomes clear that also in regard to 'tension-relaxation' one can only see a person truly and form the right opinion about his degree of development if one regards him from two levels: the worldly and the Transcendental.

By virtue of the assured participation of man's own being in the Great Being he is, even in the midst of his worldly life, still *au fond* liberated; for within his being he already *is* what he seeks. From the Christian point of view he *is* God's child and liberated through Christ. From the Eastern point of view he already *is* the Buddha-nature, he *is* in his essential substance Nirvana. But because and in so far as he has an I through which he relies upon himself and which is always turned towards the world, he is, at the same time, none of these things, but is merely on the way to uncovering them in himself. The driving force of all his seeking is nothing other than what fundamentally he already *is*. In so far as he is not all *that* in his I-world-consciousness, his essential oneness with Being shows itself as divine discontent. The separation from his Being is what produces the basic tension of his life; the release of it is imperative for the integration of his I-self with his essence. The separation from Being, painfully felt by the rigid I, is the root cause of the transcendental tension throughout men's lives. Here appears the urge of Being to manifest itself in ultimate Self, and equally the necessity of the integration of the I-self with Being.

Only if, in all efforts to achieve the right inter-action of tension and relaxation, one bears in mind that man in his innermost part is already freed, can one discover the effective guiding principle for the practice of right relaxation and right tension in his quality of citizen of this world.

To the extent that life, as mirrored by the I, takes on the character of an imaginary, conceptually ordered reality, a special system of tension and relaxation arises. Not only are all the original normal life-impulses and instinctual drives converted into goals of the will, and not only does everything a man meets set up a relation of tension with his ever self-preserving I, but in addition, through the discriminating and fixing function of the I, a special system of tension is created which needs and longs for a correspondingly special kind of relaxation. But here also something quite different is involved than merely eliminating a disturbance of the reality-pattern and life-forms created by the I; for fundamentally in every single concern of the I lies the deeper spiritual concern of the whole man—the wish to live his life according to his Being, to complete and to fulfil himself.

Thus real success in practice consists in man's liberation from these I-conditioned, persistent wrong-tensions which keep him from contact with true Being and hinder his capacity to serve it in the world. However, only where the aspirant in right relaxation *feels* in himself the unfolding of Oneness and tastes the deeply moving 'quite different' with a reverent heart and accepts it as a new *obligation* does he show that spirit which we have described as indispensible to all real practice: the spirit of *Metanoia*, where the mind is permanently turned towards the Divine. That this new relation to the divine Ground of Being should permeate the the whole life is the distant goal. Its achievement is hindered by nothing so much as by those wrong-tensions belonging peculiarly to the life and suffering of the I which have become, as it were, permanently set and crystallized.

The whole life of man is shaped by psychological burdens, some fresh and urgent, others old and of long standing; by breathtaking instinctive needs and desires as well as by self-imposed, deliberate tensions belonging to his conscious life. Without these he could not live meaningfully and effectively for one moment, and they are always there entailing a mental alertness and readiness for bodily action which is constantly present, even when for the moment his attention is not directed to any particular interest or object or goal.

All three forms of tension may be habitually so over-stressed and so deeply ingrained that they prevent the unfolding of life itself. Only the person who has at some time become really aware of them in himself and in others knows the extent to which modern man is distorted by psychological tensions and excessive mental activity. Only one who has struggled to make himself whole and sound knows how insidious the effects of those over-tensions are, and how difficult it is to free oneself from them once they have become ingrained.

Every tension represents a bent, an inclination of the living whole. In relaxation it can be eased and the whole then swings back into its rest position. In the harmonious whole tension and relaxation form an organic system complementing each other either simultaneously or in rhythmical alternation. Every tension bears the need for relaxation, every relaxation the need for tension. Always, therefore, behind this polarity the law of the whole is at work. It strives for accord and harmony and redresses every disturbing excess as soon as there is access to the compensating transcendental force coming from the ground of Being (*Seinsgrund*)—access which is blocked when the tensions have become ingrained.

What is meant by disturbance of the right relationship of tension and relaxation? We are not concerned here with physiological conditions for they also would merely point to a disturbance affecting the whole man. It is the person who is disturbed, never his body alone. What then is the disturbance of the whole person which manifests as wrong tension? It is, as a rule, nothing but a clinging to the partial which upsets the whole. As for example, the clinging to a certain position, the obsession with a certain desire, being imprisoned by a fear, the inability to get free from certain forms of aggression, resentment or compulsion. Behind all these there usually stands, consciously or unconsciously, an I held fast by a fixation.

There are two kinds of tension arising from the ego: the immediate, fleeting ones and those which have become constitutional. The former is found in all mental processes relating to any given object, in every deliberate action and in every passing emotion. The latter is a dominating wrong tension of which the sufferer is unconscious, the result of an inveterate, egocentric relation to existence. Such a permanent compulsive tension may be the result of a trauma which has passed into the body or of an inner pressure arising from a gnawing guilt or fear, a repressed need, an inability to make contact with others. In such cases the person is always in the grip of something he cannot cope with but which yet allows him to perceive his own helplessness. Such latent tensions, kept active and alive by circumstances, are heightened to breaking point whenever a complex-laden situation arises. It is an astonishing thing to see how such tensions can be wiped out at one stroke if the sufferer simply dares to let himself drop down into his vital abdominal centre and to yield to it, especially if he can be brave enough to admit that he cannot free himself from his suffering by his own efforts. It dawns on him then that the basic reason for his rigidity and strain lies in his I.

But a man may have realized for a long time that his tensions were caused by nothing but his I and its fears for its own existence. Even so he still cannot cope with the fear nor rid himself of his I. Only by learning to relax from his deepest level will he find that in full relaxation he is free of all fear. He will realize that complete depth-relaxation is the same thing as the neutralizing of the I. But the practice of deep relaxation can be significant and efficacious only when it is carried out in full awareness of its inner meaning and not merely for the relief of bodily symptoms. Only if practised in the right frame of mind does the work even of merely muscular relaxation take on its real significance. As a by-product of such practice there will indeed be an increase of efficiency and health.

The practice of relaxation begins naturally with bodily relaxation. The aspirant fixes his mind on the letting-go of the muscles of his limbs. But this by itself does not amount to much for in this way he will not arrive at the deeper meaning of relaxation. When he is able to sink himself without resistance into his limbs, which will feel heavier and heavier, he will become aware of a qualitative change in his whole state. At this point something may occur that is inwardly meaningful. An outward sign of the change of state is a temporary inability to move. This means on the one hand, that the tension necessary for response to commands from the I has left the muscles, and further, that the I has become part of a greater whole. In this state of complete relaxation something altogether new in quality can arise. It is perceived as a special kind of warmth, a sense of boundaries removed where the aspirant exists in a hitherto unknown way, lifted into an all-embracing whole, and where at the same time in a strange way, he feels safely at home within himself. From this completely conscious yet ego-less condition he returns to ordinary consciousness with one deep breath and is once more master of his limbs. If he has been deeply aware of a peculiar condition in which he no longer belonged wholly to himself and yet *was* himself in a greater sense than ever before, something of its secret power will remain alive in him. If not he will merely feel refreshed and restored physically, but nothing more— an experience of no particular interest.

What happens in the periods when an aspirant practises relaxation can bear fruit only if during the day's activities— walking, sitting, standing, performing all sorts of common actions—he keeps himself in control. In the course of real practice an organ is developed which enables the aspirant to notice instantly his wrong tensions and to correct them himself. Only if constantly tested in everyday life will Hara be experienced as the right interplay of tension and relaxation.

It is characteristic of our time that people look only for ways and means of achieving right relaxation without giving much thought to what is right tension. This perfectly reflects our entanglement in a life mechanism from which the only deliverance seems to be the total dissolving of the hard, set patterns belonging to it. But this provides no way out of the vicious circle.

Relaxation serves the inner becoming only when it is confronted by something opposing it. This is not possible when relaxation culminates in soft helpless dissolution, or when—as though it had to be that way—the aspirant, after his relaxation exercise, immediately falls back into his wrong tensions as if nothing had happened.

Right relaxation exists only where the aspirant feels that secret root from which something strives and grows without his help, which puts him and keeps him in form. It becomes evident in the practice of diaphragm-breathing as he learns to permit full exhalation and to let inhalation come of itself. This exercise, often very difficult for the beginner, gives him a freshness which is more than a mere bodily restorative. He suddenly feels again 'in form' and what is more, in one completely different from his usual tense form. The whole secret lies in this sense of 'getting back to the right form'. Purely physical relaxation exercises aim only at a mechanical relaxation of rigidity and therefore result in most cases in more slackness, the negative compensation of which is again wrong-tension.

That ground of being (*Lebensgrund*) so rarely experienced by modern man, which releases him in the right way is also the well-spring of that right tension filled with vitality which allows his unique personal form to unfold. When the right personal form appears a man has achieved his essential individuality (*Gestalt*). And not until a man perceives his own individual form—charged with its essence-tension and bringing a sense of obligation—will he understand what practice really means. And just as this true form can unfold only when the aspirant has learned to abandon the ego structure causing his wrong tensions, only then can he unfold himself fully and proudly as mind and soul. But first the I, with its false rationality, and its restless heart, must drop down into the well-spring of the Primordial Deep.

All this means that the right inter-action of relaxation and tension can come into play only when man finds his 'earth-centre' which is embodied in Hara. When he is in touch with it he will feel released and be set free for true Self-becoming. To the extent that this contact is consolidated in Hara, the waking-state-tensions necessary for normal existence in the world will be properly sustained and will become fruitful in the life sense. For one who is proficient in Hara they awaken the incentive to seek anew his contact with the healing Ground. The inter-action of wrong-tension and complete slackness will be replaced by that creative liberation from the small I which alone will allow the growth of being.

Chapter 8

The Practice of Breathing

Through breathing as through no other basic function of our life, can we realize and practise what most concerns us here. In breathing we partake unconsciously in the Greater Life. If we succeed in becoming aware of how the laws of life work out in breathing, in submitting ourselves to them consciously and in taking them in their full significance, we are already on the 'Way'. In what follows all that is said about breathing is connected with the Way.

The practice of breathing is accomplished in three stages. In the first stage it is a question of becoming conscious of the usual physical breathing, of correcting and exercising it. In the second stage the aspirant begins to recognize himself in his wrong breathing, and so to practise letting go and receiving in a new way. In the third stage he begins to recognize breathing as a sign of supernatural life and to surrender himself to it.

Right physical breathing comes from a movement of the diaphragm. If it is in order it is not the result of a doing, the breath comes and goes of itself. If the movement of the diaphragm is in any way impeded it is replaced by a movement of the auxiliary muscles located higher up. This is a sign that a person is held tightly in the circle of his I even in his breathing. Shallow breathing high up—i.e. in the chest—shows that a man is tense and caught in his I without knowing it.

The Practice of Breathing

Because the I has *to do* everything itself, such a person does not allow the breath simply to come and go, he must draw it in and he resists full exhalation. The first thing that has to be learned is *to let breathing happen*. This is possible only to the extent that a person is able to cease directing the breath from his I. Just how difficult this is becomes clear when he first observes his breathing, for then the effect of the fixing I, interrupting the natural rhythm, becomes immediately apparent. Breathing falters and the beginner frequently has the impression that he is no longer capable of breathing properly, and that he is short of breath.

It takes a long time before such a person, even one who usually breathes more or less rightly, is able to breathe consciously in the right way. To learn this is a basic exercise—*exercitium*—which is needed by both the sound and the unsound. Here, for the first time, the aspirant gets an idea of the importance of the age-old saying, 'To see as if one saw not', or 'To do without doing'. To his surprise and annoyance the beginner finds that mere knowledge of right breathing alone is of no avail. Although he already knows what is required he cannot prevent the interference of his I. Again and again he resists exhalation half-way, and half-intentionally he assists the inflowing breath. It is as if he dared not allow full exhalation and feared that he would not get enough air unless he helped. So it is a great and memorable experience when for the first time he succeeds with full consciousness, in allowing the natural, living breath to happen and discovers that it really does come and go, come and go of its own accord. Letting the breath happen without the participation of the will is therefore the first requirement. But to accomplish this the European has to learn above all to let go, to shift the point of gravity from above to below in his body, and to achieve this he usually has to learn how to let the breath flow out fully.

It might be as well here to say a word about Yoga-breathing as practised today by many people under the guidance of more or less qualified teachers. It cannot be disputed that many experience at least some temporary benefit from it. But quite often it is bad for them. If one asks why, the answer is that in rightly understood Yoga (lit: 'to yoke', i.e. 'to yoke oneself to the source of Life'), breathing is an exercise designed to assist man to find his true Self. But the self-practice leading to the ultimate Self demands something different according to the differences in the starting point of each beginner.

The Indian master in his own country deals with types of people who differ radically from people in the West. The Indian and the Oriental generally bring very different attitudes towards the practice of breathing from those brought by the Westerner. The difference is twofold: first, his whole attitude to life, and second his living conditions.

Thanks to the religious tradition of the East with its age-old roots in the practice of meditation, the practice of breathing as an exercise on the Way, is taken as a matter of course. Therefore the spiritual aspect of breathing needs hardly to be emphasized. In the same way the scripture readings, prayers and images, introducing and accompanying meditation, fall on prepared ground and are readily accepted. In the Western pupil they often cause only a vague feeling of uplift which is worthless, or at best a momentary stimulation of the mind. Only rarely do they have any permanent influence or effect on the over-all life attitude of the Western pupil. In most cases such spiritual tuning-in is soon given up altogether, and practice is then pursued only as an exercise for the body. In all this the structure of the European's total life-attitude becomes apparent.

Whereas the Indian is more in danger of sagging downwards, or of dispersing, the Westerner usually suffers from too much upward pull. Here, the danger is from too much will, there, from an inert letting-go; here too much do-it-yourself, there too much letting-it-happen; here the tendency to emphasize inhaling rather than exhaling and to hold the breath consciously; there the tendency to glide downwards and drop into a kind of unconsciousness. As certainly as the sounding-board and manifestation-field of the Absolute is the whole man, so certainly must the beginner have help in finding his own wholeness. Roughly speaking one can say that the Indian lacks the 'above'. Thus it is understandable that in Yoga-breathing emphasis is laid from the beginning on intentional inhalation and the retention of the breath at the point of completed intake. The Yoga teacher, it is true, will require the pupil at the beginning of each exercise to relax, but the teacher himself often does not realize that precisely this demands of the European what he is least able to accomplish and what he will achieve only after long practice. There are apparently only a very few Yoga teachers who watch for the self-releasing or relaxing of their Western pupils, and only then—after the pupil has really learned to let go—commence those exercises which imply tension. But in general, for the European, practice of breathing means first and foremost the step away from the intentional doing towards passive permitting. But if the European is required to begin at once with an upward-tending exercise, what happens then corresponds to his usual unconscious orientation and therefore suits and pleases him. Nonetheless it misleads him— that is, it leads to his grafting on to his ordinary, established tension, a new one produced by the new teaching. The result is at best that the Western aspirant, immediately after beginning to practice enjoys a sense of increased vitality and perhaps feels wonderfully 'fit' for a time, but later, as a consequence of the excessive demands on an ego and a will-structure already over-developed, he becomes completely supine. The artificially induced vitality is followed by a condition of exhaustion and the aspirant discontinues his efforts, his practice.

On people whose dis-ease is due to their irresoluteness and softness, their indolence and passivity, a breathing training which makes use of the will and pulls the individual upwards has only seemingly a positive effect. They cannot in truth build an effective healthy I in this way, for the healthy ego always presupposes contact with one's own being. The breathing of such usually weak and irresolute people is often shallow, and they show an anxious obscured wrong tension which has first to be dissolved before the right, vital tension from below can flow in to them. But to have no boundaries does not necessarily imply contact with the Greater Life. One who has no boundaries and who is apparently very relaxed can discover this true personal form only when he learns how to renew himself continually from the well-spring of the deep.

Purely body-training practices have little to do with Yoga in the sense of a healing and integrating work 'yoking' the individual to the ground of Being. They are only gymnastics, falsifying Yoga to methods for the increase of health, will-power and efficiency. But for his inner development a man gains nothing by them. This, however, does not alter the fact that the practice of breathing is, in the beginning, an exercise of the body which a man perceives at first only from an objective distance. In the beginning he practises something which he has 'before' him—not something which he already is as a man and a living creature. He treats not himself but his body like an instrument out of tune which he wants to re-tune and set right. In this way he acquires a certain routine which is only the foundation for what is to follow. With it comes a 'know-how' of breathing which can be very useful for general health but still does not guarantee any inner gain. The true meaning of practice begins only when the aspirant learns by means of his breathing to exercise himself, not just his body. Here lies the meaning of the second stage of the practice of breathing. And only with this does true practice begin.

At the second stage the aspirant no longer emphasizes his exhalation but learns to let himself fall into it. He no longer tries to loosen the stiff pushed-up shoulders and chest but to loosen himself. This betokens a fundamentally different approach. He learns that the wrong breathing of the body expresses a wrong attitude of his self. Not his body, but *he* breathes wrongly. Breathing is not merely an in-drawing and out-streaming of air, but a fundamental movement of a living whole, affecting the world of the body as well as the regions of soul and mind. From his breathing a man's whole attitude to life can be read. Thus the aspirant has to understand that the change concerns not only his body but his whole attitude towards himself and life. Gradually as he gains this new view of breathing he will realize the full extent of his former wrong attitude—how his faulty body posture as well as the broken rhythm of his breath were all manifestations of wrong mental attitudes which were blocking and distorting the cosmic ebb and flow of the breath of life. Wrong breathing creates resistance to the *fundamental rhythm of life* and thereby makes Self-becoming impossible.

Only a teacher or therapist who has seen time and again the fear which prevents the 'letting-oneself-fall' into the exhalation realizes that what is at work here is a fundamental lack of trust in life. The difficulty of giving up the active waking-tension of the I is rooted in the deep unconscious fear that in so doing the man will lose himself. The commonness of this fear is shown by the nervous start which many people experience just as they are dropping off to sleep—when something seems to pull the sleeper back at the very moment when he is about to surrender to the secret working of nature, in this case to the breath of sleep. What is here a strikingly obvious resistance is at other times a subtler hindrance to the blessed unconscious working of Nature, that is, being constantly on the *qui vive*, as if life's whole security and continuation depended on a man's keeping things consciously in his grip. It generally takes a long time before a beginner, turning his conscious attention to his breathing, grasps the truth that not he but 'it' breathes, and that he may confidently surrender even his breathing to the Great Power which keeps him alive without his assistance. This feeling that 'it breathes' not that 'I breathe', (and the beginner often imagines far too soon that he has known it) is one of the greatest, most impressive and most blissful experiences at the beginning of the Way.

Here a question suggests itself. Does not the individual who has never heard of breathing exercises normally surrender quite naturally to his breathing function? If so, why the exercise? The answer is that if a man did not normally surrender to it he would not live at all. But what matters on the Way is precisely becoming conscious of the life and the Being embodied in us, and this includes the becoming conscious of the basic movement of all life— which is breath. The hidden formative power of Nature takes on its fullest meaning and effect for man's higher development only when he becomes conscious of its mysterious working. *Man* matures and completes himself only by becoming conscious of those great laws which, at the level of unconscious Nature, are simply lived. But this is a special form of becoming conscious.

This special consciousness is blocked when he first begins to work because man always fixes objectively everything that he perceives from the standpoint of the I, including even himself, as soon as he observes himself carefully. As the Zen masters express it, he turns the 'inside' into an 'outside'. And thereby he alters beyond recognition what he originally wanted to perceive. Everything he fixes is at once built into the structure of his ready-made ideas and concepts, that is, into the consciousness-pattern of the I whose life-blocking outlook he wanted to transcend. 'Becoming conscious' therefore means something completely different. It is a question not of becoming intellectually or objectively conscious of the breath life and its rhythmical order as manifested in breathing, but of becoming aware of it as a living movement in which oneself is also included, without fixing it or standing apart from it.

This *awareness* of life working within us is something fundamentally different from observing, fixing and comprehending from the outside. In such observing and comprehending he who comprehends stands apart from the comprehended and observed. But in becoming *aware*, the experience remains one with the experiencer and transforms him by taking hold of him. Whenever an experience changes a person it happens unnoticed in the greater awareness of what has been experienced. To become aware means to regain the oneness with the original reality of life. A man distorts, injures and loses it because in his ego he cuts himself off from the original reality which of itself could transform him. He contradicts it by entrenching himself anew in his old thought-patterns and by trying to orient himself only by what he can pin down. Life can never be pinned down.

Letting-go of the I is unthinkable without also letting-go one's old built-in patterns of thought and consciousness. Only the dissolution of the I and all its patterns will allow the coming into force and the potential fruitfulness of that consciousness-pattern which accords with the Great Life. *This is the immanent inner consciousness.*

What matters in all practice is to lift this inner consciousness which is ordinarily the bearer of all human experience, out of its submerged secondary rôle and to give it the leading rôle. Only where the inner consciousness is re-awakened and its contents accepted can the process of becoming one (which is also conscious)—with the primordial forces of Life operate in such a way as not again to destroy this union. By becoming aware of the Source—not just 'knowing about' it—man becomes effectively aware of the estrangement into which his outer consciousness has led him, and only then will he be ready to approach and draw again from the well-springs of life.

Finding the way back to the Source is not a simple returning. Rather is this backward movement an advance to a stage where man can of his own will, freely and consciously fulfil what his nature unconsciously urges—to live life not through his ego-concepts but according to his Being. The way to this freedom leads through the development of that inward consciousness which, as distinct from all 'consciousness of something', admits life as such. Further, this active awareness of inner life is characterized by an obligating impulse of *conscience* which urges a man to live and change himself in accordance with his new realizations. Thus the spiritual awareness of breathing can never be separated from the birth of true conscience, sometimes called the Holy Wisdom.

The work of conscience bears in itself not only awareness of the valid realizations which it has called forth. It bears also a promise whose fulfilment depends on our obedience. What we become aware of in the practice of breathing can be fulfilled only in obedience to the law which we have understood in our inward consciousness.

At the second stage of the practice of breathing the aspirant must learn to free himself from the hard shell of his I as a reference point, so that he can receive himself anew and be transformed. His maturing is achieved by admitting change and transformation, loosing himself and bracing himself, opening himself and closing himself in the ready surrender of the old and the acceptance of the new. At the second stage, therefore, the aspirant must learn to lose himself in order to find himself. The I has taught him only to cling to and to preserve, never to let go and to trust. The letting-go implied here, the surrender of the I-position experienced in right breathing demands more courage than is generally supposed. And only very slowly does a man come to know himself in his hybrid self-will and his distrust of the boundless. But when at last the whole man is inspired by the breath of Life he finds in trustful self-surrender a fundamentally new confidence in life and also, in a deeper sense, he finds himself. And in this deep newly-gained trust alone can he finally win through to Himself.

It is at the third stage that he will be led to the unfathomable Void whence rises the law of the Spiritual Life.

Awareness of the life manifest in breathing is present in reality only when one senses the Great Respiration and finally keeps in rhythm with it. This means yielding oneself without reservation to the cosmic movement of ebb and flow. One must understand from the core of one's being that all forms are brought forth in stillness and when they are fulfilled, taken back again. Man as a creature is also subject to this law of life. But to the extent that he has developed only his specifically human consciousness, he confronts this cycle of dying and becoming, passing away and rising again with his ordinary will to cling to life. And the result of this will is a hardening, a lack of permeability which causes the Great Life in him to suffocate. When a man experiences for the first time that his breath, hitherto so narrow and small, permeates him completely and lifts him joyously into abundance, he tastes his new living wholeness and his significant belonging to a Greater Life. It is in the progressive unfolding of this inner experience that man enters the Great Way.

On the way to re-rooting himself in the ground of Life the aspirant has already, at the second stage of practice, taken an essential step forward. It is the step towards lightening and making more penetrable the hard shell of his ego. He has already begun to rise above that level of consciousness in which he perceived his own body only as a thing. But the development which is to root him anew in the Primal Life would be arrested half-way if the experience were no more than a feeling of agreeable release from confining barriers. Ultimately what matters is not that a man should liberate himself but that he should enter the Great Life with the understanding that his Self-being is a responsible *participation* in the Great Life. The breathing practice leading to this stage is that of trustful and obedient yielding, deliberately, attentively listening. From such a yielding he returns not only as a more clear-sighted I-self but as a witness of that to which he has surrendered.

The meaning of the second stage is realized when man has acquired the assurance that if he loses himself he will find *himself* again. The meaning of the third stage is the blissful, convincing and binding experience of participation in the *Whole*. At the first stage breathing is practised involuntarily as something belonging to the outer world. At the second stage man practises himself, and finds himself safely within himself. But at the third stage it is neither the one nor the other, for here a new life-impulse breaks through which has transcended the opposites and which sets a man on a new path. At this stage, where a man in his practice revolves neither round an object nor round himself but around a completely new centre-of-meaning, that religious feeling develops which lives neither by ideas nor by mystical feeling, but which is the expression of the creative and liberating working of the divine being arising within the human self.

What have the three stages of breathing to do with the practice of Hara? Neither more nor less than that they all serve the attainment of the 'earth centre' which allows progress in practice, and which then leads on to still higher levels of human development. With the strengthening of Hara comes the courage necessary for the complete abandonment of the ego which enables a man progressively to anchor himself in that centre where the Primordial arises.

The advance from one stage to the next implies a growing possibility of reaching the true Self. In the beginning there is the 'I am I', possessing a body which breathes wrongly and which must learn to breathe rightly. Then comes the growth of that greater I-self that feels at one with his original soul-body (*Ur-Lieb*), when he experiences himself as a human being individually connected with the Great Breath of Life. And finally comes the supreme experience of the 'I am' in the sense of total participation in the Greater Life whose breath leads the aspirant homewards, born anew. In the course of this transformation, the whole centre of gravity has shifted downward and Hara is so well developed that its strength enables a man then on to live his daily life from the breath of the Great Life.

So much for the purpose and the manner of the earliest Hara-practice leading to that level of development which, by a backward movement, restores a man to the ground-root of Being. But even the little that has been said of the nature and practice of Hara can be understood only by one who has already begun to practise. To anyone without personal experience, what we have said about the results of Hara-practice must necessarily seem exaggerated and improbable, all the more so since the inexperienced, as we have said before, are always in danger of regarding it as a merely physical exercise unrelated to the needs of the mind and soul. Also the inexperienced invariably tend to under-estimate the heavy demands made by genuine practice. The exercises taken separately may be easy, but to become one who practises is not.

The practice of Hara, cannot be limited to certain hours of the day for such practice helps only to acquire right posture, a feeling for the right balance of tension and relaxation, and the training in right breathing. The daily period of practice develops an inner organ which enables the aspirant to become aware immediately of every wrong posture in his daily life and to correct himself. But the full meaning of practice is reached only when it has become a constant force penetrating the whole of everyday life.

Accordingly, we should now try to point out what Hara means in the basic, recurring situations of ordinary life. We should show separately how it affects a person in physical or mental work, in creative activity, in love, in his relations with his fellow-men, in his work, in the planning of his life and in the acceptance of his destiny. But all this would require a deeper penetration into still wider spheres of thought which will be dealt with in a later book. So far we have spoken of Hara exclusively as the expression of man's basic earth-centre and shown the immediate effects of possessing it. To continue would mean to enlarge further upon the higher reaches of mental and spiritual development possible only to those firmly anchored in the regained earth-centre. But to indicate such possibilities is a task of supreme importance for our time.

We stand today in the radiance of a new burst of light from that transcendental Being which underlies our human life as conditioned by space and time, in the sign of a re-discovery of the laws of the Greater Life amidst the contingencies of our little life between birth and death. In this opening of completely new vistas the regaining of contact with the Primordial Ground is only the first part of the task. The real task lies in the shaping of life by the spirit. The indispensible condition of this is the rediscovery of the first principles of that *Mind* which manifests Primordial Oneness. Only in this movement of the spirit will we comprehend the full significance of the releasing, sustaining and creative earth-centre, which is Hara.

V
Retrospect and Outlook

Chapter 9

Retrospect and Outlook

When a man starts to consider his life he realizes that his standing in the world is a twofold one. He finds himself in his historical actual world and at the same time feels himself linked in his innermost being to an extra-historical Greater Life. To live in the world, and not merely to exist, but to live significantly and happily, he needs the strength to make his way and to secure his position in life, he needs to know and understand things, to build on right values and he needs the capacity to love. To the extent that he confronts the risks, the disorder and the lovelessness of life only with the strength of his will and intellect, and as long as his emotions are predominantly conditioned by the 'world', sooner or later he comes to a barrier. Then follows the foredoomed suffering of mankind which, blinded by its exclusive preoccupation with the world of time and space, has lost sight of the way inwards.

Man's 'way inwards' is the way of uniting himself with his *Being* wherein he partakes of Life beyond space and time. This is the way to maturity, the way that yields fruit in proportion to his success in integrating 'himself' with his Self.

There is an inherent obstacle on the way inwards which threatens even the sound healthy man, namely, that by the very structure of his consciousness, may assume complete control of the man's whole life. The door to the inner life can then re-open only when a man is able to break through the domination of the I and win contact with that Being and Life within him which evades all his 'arrangements'. But only an established inner attitude enabling him constantly, from within this world, to participate in the Great Being will bring him the fruit of this integration. For only by his capacity to live and prove the Greater Life in the lesser one, only in the manifestation of Being in the world can man fulfil his appointed destiny as the simpler creatures do.

The way inwards rests on three factors. The first is an *experience* wherein the light of Being illuminates the darkness of life. The second is *insight* into the relationship of his worldly I and his transcendental Being, as well as into the difference between the state in which he is cut off from his Being and the right state which opens him to it. The third is *practice*, *exercitium*, which corrects the wrong working of the misguided I and builds up the right attitude in a right way. That is a right attitude in which a man is permeable to the Greater Life which he embodies and by which he is enabled to perceive it in the world. He is then truly himself and the world of space and time becomes transparent for him in the Being which transcends space and time.

The way leading to this condition is by the transformation of the *whole* man, i.e. a unit of body, mind and soul. What keeps man estranged from Being consists not only in his being fettered by psychological complexes and by the rigidity of his thought-patterns, but also by the fact that they are fixed in his flesh and set fast in wrong bodily habits. So any renewal can be achieved only through the transformation of the whole man, and implies not only an intellectual and spiritual conversion, but also a transformation of the body and all its postures and movements. Without this bodily transformation all inner experience of Being comes to a standstill when the experience has passed, and the man inevitably falls victim again to his old, familiar fixing and classifying consciousness. Therefore practice must inevitably include practice of the body.

Just as the right inner state is clearly expressed in the symbolism of the harmoniously functioning body, so inner malformations appear as bodily malformations. These have one thing in common: lack of centre. Lack of centre implies either that a man is anchored too firmly in his upper body or that he lacks anchorage altogether. Only where a firm middle region exists is man's entire psycho-physical state properly entred.

The whole life attitude of a human being appears in his posture, in the relationship of tension and relaxation, and in breathing. Posture, tension and relaxation, and breath can never be exclusively physical factors. They are integral functions of the person manifesting himself analogously on the psychological and spiritual levels. For this reason it is possible to begin the work on the whole man with them.

One can speak of 'right' training in posture, relaxation and breathing only when it is undertaken in the service of Self-becoming. Efficiency in the world is indeed a fruit of integration with Being, but this is not the primary aim of practice understood as *exercitium*. Actually integration with Being becomes more difficult if posture, relaxation and breathing exercises are directed only towards a man's relation to the world, for precisely because they will strengthen him in his illusory autonomy and life-efficiency, they will serve too to support and increase his estrangement from Being.

The poverty of man's relation to Being is shown by the malformed I. There are two extreme cases of malformation —in the one a man is encased in an impenetrably hard I-shell, in the other he has no I-covering whatever. Once the I has been injured there is no 'worldly' remedy to free a man from his fears, despairs and sorrows and to help him re-discover the support, trust and sense of protection which he needs. Only on the way which gives him back again his innate contact with Being, the loss of which is expressed in his impotence and suffering, can he become whole again.

Becoming one with Being means transcending the structure patterns of ordinary consciousness. Therefore there can be no re-anchoring in Being as long as experience, insight and practice do not break through the narrow circle of the usual rational consciousness-pattern. All the struggling to acquire knowledge, all practice which merely strengthens the will, and all efforts to put feeling under discipline are doomed to failure when the Transcendental is the goal. A man has to overcome the dichotomy of objective and sub-jective consciousness, to let the original Unity penetrate his awareness and to let himself be embraced by it without wanting or trying to understand and hold it. When he admits the primal Unity which was within him before and beyond all I-becoming he will find true renewal. By dropping his ego and submerging himself in the Primordial Life he will find Being within himself, become more and more at one with it, become through never flagging practice truly new, and as a renewed being *prove* himself as a witness of the Great Being.

The inner movement from 'I' to the 'It' as seen in the symbolism of the body and in the ascent from unconscious Nature to the rational I consciousness, is a 'backward movement'. The powers of the I-intellect, will and emotion—are located in the upper part of the body. Their working 'on their own' shows in a centre of gravity too high up, in being tensed upwards and in upper-body breathing. To be released from this exclusively upward pull there is but one remedy, letting oneself drop downwards and anchoring oneself in Hara. Hara, literally translated belly, means indeed the physical belly but this understanding of it in the merely bodily sense exists only in the view of the I which automatically separates body and soul. Hara implies actually the *whole man* in full contact with the nourishing, begetting, conceiving, carrying and re-generating root-forces of life. Hara is the region where the Primal Oneness of life is to be found. When a man can preserve his union with it under all circumstances he will remain completely at one with the Great Life within him.

To the extent that the whole man, in the course of his becoming conscious, identifies himself with the I and identifies his world with his consciousness—to that extent he estranges himself from his Being. Helplessly exposed to the tensions of life always perceived solely through the pairs of opposites, he loses the blessedness inherent in the Original One. But if he is able to subordinate his I and to re-root himself in his earth-centre, the yoke of the I is lightened and the forces of the deep arise within him. For the I-imprisoned the finding of these forces in Hara means the ability to give up his cherished stand in the realm of the ego and the finding of a different foothold—a longed for release. For him who lacks a firm I-base it means the discovery of a power which consolidates him and shapes him from within. Finding himself in Hara means then two things: liberation from the wrong I, the one not in contact with Being and hence from the pseudo-self, and the opening of a way to the right I, which is in contact with Being, and ultimately to the true Self.

In this finding of Hara something decisive has happened. Gone is the dependence on the world, which has been regarded as the sole reality but where the I-will finally founders, where the I-spirit never finds a satisfying world-order and where the I-heart remains forever enmeshed in suffering. In its place is the All-in-All where every contradiction is resolved and all space-time reality loses its significance. But this represents an advanced applying stage only to one who regards the I-reality as a mere delusion and the lifting of this delusion as an *ultimate* goal.

For the Westerner, also, if he progresses on the inner way, the world anchored in the I becomes a delusion. But it remains delusion for him only as long as his 'I-reality' preserves its absolute character as the *only* reality. It ceases to be a delusion as soon as he is able to recognize it as the *medium* through which true Reality shows itself. Then the I-reality becomes transparent to Being and also the sphere of manifestation for him who bears within himself the One. The new man then constantly perceives the One in all colours, images and patterns through which Being is refracted in the prism of the I. To realize Being in all and everything then becomes the sole function of his life. Time is no longer opposed to eternity but is the medium which reflects it. 'Everything in space and time *means* ultimately only Eternity.'

In this European or, more specifically, Christian view, a personal experiencing of the One is in fact only the beginning of the way of ultimate transformation. It is true that already in the never-ending discovery and re-discovery of that centre of the primal Unity in man, new horizons open for the mind and new depths for the heart. But, when man lifts himself from the earth-centre of his human nature to the heaven-centre of his spirit and when, in his heart-centre he joyously accepts the obligation to actualize the Original Unity and its inherent order within his existence in this world, then will his insight and practice flow out in one stream of true creative activity on earth. For the Kingdom of Heaven on earth is our true heritage and only within it will the real 'circulation of light' be established.

Japanese Texts

Chapter 1

Okada Torajiro

Introduction

Master Okada Torajiro worked during the first two decades of this century. Many of his pupils, then students, have attained high official positions. One of them, Count F. told me the following story from his youth. 'When I was studying at the Tedai (the Imperial University) about 1910 it was the time when intellectualism in academic education was at its peak. We were overfed with rationalism. The lectures frequently consisted of nothing but recited translations from Western books. We found nothing that moved us, that touched our nature, so to speak. But there was Master Okada who, we were told, had said "If you come and practice with me you will not, it is true, accumulate knowledge, but you will learn to understand the speech of birds."

'Many of us went to him very early in the morning. We would get up at five o'clock to "sit" with Master Okada before our lectures began. In the bitter winter weather this was often hard but we were keen and we went. Little was said. Mostly the Master just "sat" with us, corrected our postures, scarcely speaking. But we gained much and today I still know that I am infinitely indebted to him for this work.' It is an interesting fact that everyone considers Count F. to be about fifteen years younger than he actually is.

Another, a man of great physical and mental vitality, Ambassador K. told me (he was then over sixty) that as a young man he had been weak and sickly and that he owed it exclusively to Seiza[1] that he was now fresh, vigorous and in excellent health. These are but two examples out of many.

After Master Okada's early death his work was carried on by a woman, Dr Kobayashi, with whom I had the opportunity of practising Seiza. She also gave me the little book 'Words of the Master' to keep with me always on my way.

[1] *Seiza*—the practice of 'sitting' and nothing more as taught by Okada.

Hara

Quite uncomplicated directions are typical of the methods of the Japanese masters. The master rarely speaks, he demonstrates. The pupil adapts himself to an atmosphere and imitates the master as best he can—over and over again. From time to time a quick correction drops into the silence. Madame Kobayashi's method—as far as I could see—was for the most part simply to sit or kneel opposite her pupil at a distance of some thirty inches, while she herself simply 'practised' for half an hour. I remember how, at my second session with her I had tried during the half hour of my practice to keep my eyes open. She realized this only at the end of the period and then, seeing that my eyes had watered, told me that I might just keep them closed for the time being. This wordless teaching coming out of the silence and the silent action makes a very strange impression. Only now and then during the following lessons came a light word, a silent gesture, a light touch on my shoulders or head, a quick pressure at the small of my back.

In what follows I give a translation of some of the sayings of Master Okada. The sequence is not that of the original but is here arranged according to subject-matter.

Sayings of Master Okada

Tanden[1] is the shrine of the Divine. If its stronghold is finely built so that the Divine in us can grow then a real human being is achieved. If one divides people into ranks the lowest is he who values his head. Those who endeavour only to amass as much knowledge as possible grow heads that become bigger and so they topple over easily, like a pyramid standing upside down. They excel in imitating others but neither originality nor inventiveness nor any great work is theirs.

Next come those of middle rank. For them the chest is most important. People with self-control, given to abstinence and asceticism belong to this type. These are the men with outward courage but without real strength. Many of the so-called great men are in this category. Yet all this is not enough.

But those who regard the belly as the most important part and so have built the stronghold where the Divine can grow—these are the people of the highest rank. They have

[1] Tanden—region about two inches below the navel.

developed their minds as well as their bodies in the right way. Strength flows out from them and produces a spiritual condition of ease and equanimity. They do what seems good to them without violating any law. Those in the first category think that Science can rule Nature. Those in the second have apparent courage and discipline and they know how to fight. Those in the third know what reality is.

Seiza makes use of the posture most certain to produce people of the third category. The sorrows of humanity are caused by loss of balance. To preserve it one has to have a healthy body and an upright heart. These can be achieved only 'on the way'. To reach the way means 'sitting'! If you 'sit' for two or three years you will understand.

From getting-up time until bedtime you must be awake (on the jump). Keep your posture in Hara, come what may, and you will be alert in the right way.

You sit for one year, two years, three years, and you think—and so do others—that you are like one born anew. In truth however you are just a little shoot on the way to the development of your being. It takes fifty to sixty years to become like the heaven-striving cedars and cypresses.

Even if the body is changed in Seiza the deepest inner state does not change so quickly.

Keep a carp in a pond with a stone in the centre and another of equal size with nothing in the centre. In the pond where the stone is the carp swims round the stone all the time and thus has its exercise without meeting resistance. He grows more quickly than the carp in the other pond. This is the result of endless repetition.

What is Seiza?
Before I am, thou art, he is—is that.... ! To know that is Seiza.

Hara

Christ said, 'Unless ye become as little children ye cannot enter the kingdom of Heaven.' That is true. The same applies to Seiza.

Seiza aims at the perfection of human being. The achievement of health and the acquisition of healing powers are secondary factors.

People did not know before that there was a method of developing intelligence, physical health and morality all at the same time. Therefore they laughed at my teaching.

There were people who thought that Seiza was a kind of hypnotism. But Seiza is not that. On the contrary, Seiza implies such a development that one will never fall under the power of hypnotism no matter how strong it may be.

On Breathing

Seiza is the master and breath the serving-man. Breathing is a means of achieving Seiza. Therefore Seiza is the more important. But both, Seiza and breath, are means of developing mind and body. Their operation is fulfilled in faith.

Some say that it is a kind of health-breathing, others that it is a new religion. And there are many other views. But none is correct, and all that merely makes me laugh. But one day it will probably become a great question for learned circles and then my aim will become clear. Until then I'll leave it at that.

Sit quite still, breathe gently, giving out long breaths, the strength in the lower belly.

Only because there is no strength in the belly does one get out of breath when running.

He who swims with Hara will make good speed.

Nowadays a soldier is allowed to sleep with his mouth open. In olden times he would soon have been done for.

Breathing through the mouth is a sign of decline.

When a fish is dying he puts his big mouth above the surface of the water and gasps for air.

Many of our people breathe through their mouths. But the whole people should breathe through the nose and press the breath down into the tanden.

Tanden breathing is the beginning of tanden practice and the foundation of Seiza. With each breath one should gather one's whole strength in the tanden.

When exhaling one should not give out the breath entirely. One should keep enough back to enable one to speak a few words.

One breath after the other with the whole body strength of tanden—this is like a chisel which gradually shapes up all the muscles fully, organically.

Always, even when climbing a precipice, one should exhale very slowly at the same time pressing strength into the tanden. Let us repeat—to strengthen Hara, long, slow out-breathing. As if emptying a pump one must press his breath down into the belly. Most people lack this training in every day life. So they know nothing about gathering strength in the belly. Nor can they keep their mouths firmly shut.

Make the exhalation long. In olden time a knight crossed the Ryohgoku bridge during the time of one breath. I have

179

seen fisherwomen who when diving could hold their breath for many minutes. In a Chinese book it is said that one should cool oneself by staying half a day under water. And there is also a story of a shipwrecked man who was under water for days before he was brought up in a net. Then only did he draw breath.

For inhaling a moment is enough.

The study of breath is of the greatest significance. Even *ninjutsu*, the art of making oneself invisible and other ancient arts come from the mastery of breathing.

Ordinary people breathe eighteen times a minute. Less than ten are sufficient for those who practise Seiza. But if one can manage with three a minute it is really good.

Someone asked whether he would make progress if he stayed in the country for a year and worked with Dr Kobayashi. 'Yes, if you have got beyond the boundaries of happiness and ambition then you will be able to develop yourself.'

A difference of a hair's breadth (with his hand on a pupil's body) and already there is a split between heaven and earth. But the unity that is—before 'heaven and earth' were—is what matters.

Let the heart of the whole body be completely empty and only here (pointing with his finger to the pupil's tanden) let there be strength.

The Seiza posture is in accord with nature. Why does a five-storey pagoda not collapse? Because it keeps its physical balance. If one sits in the Seiza posture one does not topple over no matter from which side one may be pushed.

Like a five-storey pagoda—so faultless should your posture be.

Gather your strength in one point only—in the lower belly.

In your head is no tanden. Do not put so much strength in your head.

It is useless if you cannot keep it up for thirty minutes.

Keep the trunk erect. Hands folded and lightly pressed on the belly.

The trunk (*koshi*) should be taut and firm.

When the base is strong the extremities are easily controlled.

Do not try to free yourself from all thoughts. Simply be watchful and keep your strength in your belly.

Why is one unshakable in the Seiza posture? Because the foundation-stone is firm and fixed. A trunk held well erect shows that the spine is not out of line.

Letting force (tension) out of the pit of the stomach does not mean that it should be soft when the tanden is being filled. Of course it becomes somewhat firm. Only it should never be swollen and hard.

Do not keep the mouth open. Let the neck touch the back of the collar.

When the perpendicular of the body holds firm the perpendicular of the mind is also firm. Relaxed quiet and bold force both have their source here.

Hara

There must be strength in the eyes.

Blinking is not good, it weakens the nerves.

There are people who half close their eyes when they go into the summer sunshine. They are weak people.

One should be able to keep one's eyes wide open even when looking straight into the sun.

Push your back collar stud out.

If one takes care only to pull in the chin paying no attention to the pit of the stomach and to the trunk, the chest will gradually protrude.

When the chest protrudes a person becomes obstinate and selfish—self-centred.

Your posture is twisted because your minds are twisted.

The feet are the kindling, and the belly the stove.

You should always have your head cool and your feet warm.

When there is no force in the tanden the head gets hot and the feet get cold. The hot-headed and the cold-footed is either over sensitive or ill. Such people do not have themselves in hand.

A man of strong body and peaceful feeling will certainly have a cool head and warm feet. He has his strength from Hara.

Learning and Teaching
Knowledge of the ways of the world cannot be won by

ordered, logical thinking. If one can 'look' into that true knowledge which arises from the body's centre one will understand the ultimate meaning of all the world's appearances.

Nowadays the way of educating as well as the way of learning is wrong. True knowledge is not in the written word. Books are always 'translations'. The 'original' is what *is* by its own nature.

It has never occurred to me to keep in my head what I have read. If I merely 'read' the Bible or Buddhist books and prayers I find there only such things as agree with my own thoughts.

To make others remember what has been given to them is not education. The creative force which invents, discovers and begins something new—the release of this force is education. Creative force? That is the in-dwelling Divine. Creative force results from the development of the Divine in us—including our bodies.

What a pale face! If you practice yet look pale, and you don't begin to like a dish you disliked before your work has been useless. Such practice is good for dying but not for living. Take unto yourself real learning and thenceforth you will live happily.

Look to it to be taught as little as possible. If you 'sit' you will understand quite by yourself.

Seiza as practised by teachers in ordinary schools is completely unsuccessful. This is due to the fact that they practise Seiza as though it were a course of training of which they learn a little and then straightway pass on the little they have learned.

You should never (when sitting) think about concentration of mind or even try to achieve clear purity of mind.

(Against the danger of form.) You must be able to see the face of the child that was there even before it was conceived in its mother's womb. In the past I never thought about the 'form' of sitting. And what I mean could perhaps be shown more easily through dancing than through Seiza. Therefore do not be too concerned with form.

Seiza means to teach children as yet unborn, to influence them without any pre-conceived picture (idea). How could one want to give children still unborn the Seiza form?

You must understand what the rice and the corn say. To raise rice and corn and to bring up children is, in principle, one and the same thing. Can you let rice and corn 'sit'?

The true meaning of education is to draw out the natural essence (original nature) of the individual. This leads also to the perfecting of the personality and the awakening of the soul.

Enthusiasm and ecstasy? These make the blood rush to the head. But when practising Seiza one should keep one's head quiet and cool.

A cypress increases its rings even as a very old tree. One should grow indeed until the moment of death.

Therapeutics
There are people whose eyes begin to fail. Because of the cornea? For three months they may go to an eye specialist. What nonsense! If they are made to do exercises with their eyes, not only will their eyes be spoiled their lives will be endangered. They maintain that their eyes are bad. Funda-

mentally, however, it is their minds which are not in order. If their minds are healed their eyes will be healed in a perfectly natural way. If they will 'sit' constantly for three months their eyes will be all right again. The good doctor is within themselves.

An old woman felt sharp pains in her hips during the Seiza posture. She thought she was suffering from a bone disease. Later, to her great surprise, she realized that she was completely healed.

'Sitting' in a room next to that of a mentally disturbed person will produce a change, a transformation in that person.

Why do your feet ache? Because there is no force in your lower belly.

(To one whose hands were too cold.) It is because you are putting no strength in your lower belly.

'I have such a headache.' No answer. 'Oh! the back of my head!' Still no answer. Then, in a deep voice, 'Try sitting, and watch.'

Kurosegawa (a *sumō* wrestler) fell ill though it was part of his profession always to be in training. For a long time he found no cure. After sitting for two weeks he was healed. Good eating and sport by themselves are useless.

The weaker one is the less appetite one has and the more one desires 'tasty' food. Rough food must become for us a feast.

The meaning of all things is within, in the 'mind', not something which exists 'out there'.

Hara

One who always fears that his honour is going to be offended is weaker than the person who offends him. One who is disturbed by dust is weaker than dust. And one who is frightened of germs is weaker than germs.

Strong people cannot be disturbed by anything. They may have weak intestines, fever, consumptive lungs and yet they are healthy because they are never in the least unquiet.

Even if one lung is diseased and the other gets stronger and does three times as much work as the diseased one, does that not indicate more strength?

One whose *ki* (mind) is in disorder is called *byoki* which means troubled, disturbed mind.

Be interested in the universe. Do not cling to this world. Do not want to possess anything. Never think of your 'pension'.

Mrs X. has given away her diamond ring. But what, after all, is a ring? If she did not cling to her life she could be happy.

Seiza means to give up one's 'I'.

When one sits, a good meal and a good bed are being prepared. The good cook and the good mattress are within oneself. When one sits, a lovely cool wind blows in summer, and in winter a cosy fire burns on the hearth. The cool wind and the warm hearth are within oneself.

The soldier stands in absolute obedience before one who is, after all, only one rank above him. If one masters Seiza one can stand calmly before anyone.

'The way'—it is within oneself. If one goes on sitting quietly the way will be revealed.

I have met all my misfortunes as though they were my honoured teachers. Therefore I have no place for pity towards anyone who complains, no matter how unhappy he may be.

It is a bad sign to grow thin when one meets misfortune. The deeper the sorrow the better the appetite should be and the more one should put on weight.

Never will you reach the way unless you live in the Absolute and away from relativity.

The foundation of all education is love. This love is not the one whose opposite is hate but the love that is like sunshine. Practise Seiza and you will experience it.

It is not that only after you have practised you reach. . . . The state of . . . is even now, since you 'sit'.

Result and Effect
Until the voice and the eyes alter one cannot say that one has sat in the right way.

The voice must come from the belly.

Patience, self-discipline and perseverance—he who does not use these words in this world, and he who feels Spring everywhere in heaven and in earth—one who has reached this state of mind has really understood.

If there is no strength in the tanden, vices such as

jealousy, envy, wrath, greed and distrust appear.

Pride, laziness, moodiness, suspiciousness—all these come from lack of force in the belly.

Practice in such a way that nobody will ever again be able to constrain you. You should not alter when circumstances alter. In all that concerns the way you should show yourselves incapable of being led astray.

The whole of creation is mine. All books are merely translations of my mind. Seiza is the original of all books and the eternal Spring. Are books then no longer necessary? One cannot say that. By reading one can see how far one has progressed. That applies to all practice.

The fool and the clever man are equally worthy of veneration when the divine light strikes them.

Once you have entered the way, philosophy is no longer difficult. Philosophy, so-called, becomes commonplace once you have Seiza.

Seiza sets people free.

The really blissful life—not wonderful food and beautiful women, but unlimited love for primordial Nature.

One may have second sight. But trying to preserve it destroys one's health. It is the devil's way.

I—he—you— what that means you will grasp only when you grasp what . . . is.

Feel yourself as rich as a king. On the way everyone can be happy even if he is a beggar.

Okada Torajiro

Every man has *reichi*—divine wisdom, and *reinoh*—divine power—within himself.

Before I—you—he—exists, there is. . . . To have this inwardly—that is Seiza.

Chapter 2

Sato Tsuji: The Teaching of the Human Body

Introduction

Sato Tsuji is a contemporary Japanese philosopher with a wide knowledge of Western philosophy. But for him, in accordance with Eastern tradition, philosophy means more than a clarification of human existence by means of thought. It means a realization 'with the body' of what has been understood.

Man's body, as distinct from the bodies of inanimate objects and the animal bodies of other living creatures, is the 'embodiment of the combined functions of the active self'. He says, 'Man is only in his lowest dimension a material body, a thing, an object. In his next dimension he is at the same time an animal body, a flesh body. But as a human body he is endowed with an autonomous mind, forming with it, an inseparable unity. The specifically human body is the vessel of the Way, and what it teaches us is the teaching of the Way which can be realized only with the whole body.

'The human body *in its essence* is a Dharma body, a Logos body. It is a concrete revelation of the Dharma.' And only in so far as man lives out with his body the great law of Life inherent in him, can he fulfil his appointed destiny.

According to Sato Tsuji, 'It is the fateful error of Western philosophers that they always regard the human body intellectually, from the outside, as though it were not indissolubly a part of the active self.'

We give below some excerpts from Sato Tsuji's work, *The Teaching of the Human Body* which refer to Hara. The achievement of a centre of gravity in Hara and everything connected with it is the cardinal point of Tsuji's philosophy. From the physical point of view it is the co-ordinating centre of the animal body. In its human significance it is indeed also a point. But in this case it is to be understood as a 'primordial source of strength', not as a position to be placed anatomically. It is the seat of life, not to be perceived externally but to be known from within.

Excerpts from Sato Tsuji (considerably abridged in translation)
The Self that has fully attained to itself is shown by an autonomous denial or resistance to the gravitational pull of the earth. A thing is completely dominated by the force of gravity. The animal body automatically overcomes the domination of the force of gravity. The human-self-body in its denial of the gravitational pull of earth is the expression of an autonomous will. The nature of this self-body is shown by its freedom of movement and by the uprightness of the trunk.

If the true mark of the human being is the uprightness of his body, then the character of *man* must be expressed by an intentional actualization of this posture. To maintain it the tension of will-power is necessary. When this slackens, the loins become weak and man falls into a posture in which the region of the stomach and abdomen are compressed. Thus it is absolutely necessary to maintain the lumbar vertebrae upright by will otherwise they give way and bend under the weight of the upper body. This posture indicates that the lowest, most material mode has prevailed and the active self has become passive.

The most important, the strongest and also the most sensitive part of the body and hence of the body-soul (body-Self) unity is called the *kyusho*. It lies in the whole of the trunk below the level of the navel. This region is called the *koshi*. Hence the self-supporting principle is rooted in the *koshi*. If the koshi is not filled with force the body no longer contains a centre of strength in itself and it will then be drawn downwards by a force exterior to itself, i.e. by the gravitational pull of the earth. The limbs then cease to co-ordinate. The body loses its significance as an independent, self-enclosed life.

A strong upright koshi is an affirmation of the active bodily constitution of the human being. If the upper body is heavy and the lower body (weak) it shows that the lower materiality predominates over the higher. Contrariwise, a heavy lower body connected with a light upper body indicates a life of individual character which yet comprises the lower materiality. Only this corresponds to the true logic of life. And the physiological norm accords with it.

If one keeps the trunk erect and allows the koshi to be heavy the circulation of the blood in the lower body is stimulated and one is warm. Cool head, warm feet—from olden times these were considered signs of good health, where as hot head and cold feet, cold loins and a cold bottom were always signs of poor health. Hakuin Zenshi says, 'The way to care for the living consists of keeping the upper body cool and fresh, the lower body warm.'

To achieve the right posture one must first fill the lower belly with the strength of the whole body. To fill the *koshi* with strength means also to tense the abdominal muscles a little. If one tenses the abdominal muscles in the right way there appears, as a result of this tension, a point of concentration below the navel. This point is the centre of man as a human-body-unity. It is called the tanden. The art of activating it is to release the strength of all the other parts of the body and to concentrate it there. This art since ancient times has been cultivated in *budo*, the way of the knight, in *gedo*, the way of the artist and in *sado*, the way of sitting.

The point which is the seat of the subject in the human body, must be realized inwardly. Just as the subject cannot be seen from outside this point cannt be recognized as something anatomical. A *subject* can never be made the *object* of recognition. Thus the centre of gravity of the earth, understood as a living being which is the seat of the 'One', and through which the earth becomes the One, can, insofar as this centre of gravity reflects the subject of the earth, never be made the object of recognition.

The method of looking inward which Hakuin Zenshi taught consists in the aspirant lying down, stretching his legs straight out, holding them firmly close together and in gathering the strength of the whole body into the middle. This method of Hakuin is very well calculated to put the whole body 'into one'. If one stretches the knee muscles and puts strength into the legs and into the *koshi*, one feels with delight how the whole body is filled with strength. Then one should withdraw the strength from the legs and take it back into the *koshi*, and, in this way, practice feeling the strength in the *koshi* alone.

As soon as the man gets to his feet his centre of gravity comes into evidence. Now the art of looking inward must be practised in the upright posture. First it is necessary to place the feet firmly on the ground and let the soles be, so to speak, glued to it. At the same time one must stretch the knee-muscles and put one's strength into the legs. Then the legs become firm as a tree-trunk and the *koshi* of itself will fill with strength. Then the strength must be withdrawn from the legs and taken back into the koshi. Then when all the strength is gathered into the *koshi* one places the feet on the ground by the strength of the *koshi*.

Filling the *koshi* with strength goes naturally hand in hand with breathing out. While inhaling one must withdraw the strength from the belly but, at the same time, maintain the right condition of the *koshi*. Then the inhaled air enters by itself and fills the upper belly. At the end of the inhalation the lower Hara becomes strong by itself and one can then quite naturally and smoothly change over to exhaling. The change from inhaling to exhaling and vice versa must be completely smooth and one must not interrupt the breathing during the change over.

Hara

When all the muscles of the body attain their right balance the region of the stomach becomes concave during exhalation but the lower belly curves slightly outward. This does not mean that one should thrust it out purposely. The volume and contour of the lower part of the body seen from outside changes very little, but it fills out firmly. Thus the lower part of the body effects the change from emptiness to fullness although its volume alters only very slightly.

In this exercise inhalation is short, whereas exhalation is long, since the Hara is being re-inforced. But this does not mean that one should economize with the air to be exhaled. One should pull the chin in slightly, open wide the floor of Hara and expel the air fully and strongly. This exhalation must, when nearing its end, become thicker, like a club. If the floor of Hara is devoid of strength exhalation is superficial and wheezy, but if one really breathes from it the breathing becomes powerful and flowing.

The lower belly and the buttocks complement each other as the front and back of the base of the trunk, and in this way they constitute a special unity. The strength of the *koshi* is one which makes a firm base of the trunk. Letting the strength flow into the *koshi* means, therefore, either to keep the buttocks heavy or to make the lower abdomen firm. If the buttocks are pressed back and the lower abdomen is tensed forward the base of the trunk is as firm as a rock. The hip bone then stands firm between the buttocks and the lower belly forming a true body perpendicular.

Letting strength flow into the tanden does not mean thrusting the weight of the upper body on to the lower body. When one lets the strength flow into the *koshi*, the lower body, carrying the upper part of the body, gains as it were a 'nominative' character. It would therefore be a mistake to look for the source of strength in the *koshi* in the upper part of the body. If one were to press the strength actively into the tanden by 'squashing' it, the body would become bent and lose its natural form and the upper part of the body would still remain *master* of the body. The strength filling the *koshi* should in fact be a strength which acts as if the upper part of the body did not exist at all. Therefore one should gather the strength of the whole body into the base of the trunk as if the body-perpendicular grew straight up from the centre of the earth. The koshi carries the upper part of the body with a strength striving upward from below. When strength lies in the tanden the buttocks are also contracted.

In wrong postures the trunk is only apparently supported but actually the body tends to lean back and keeps upright only with difficulty. That means that the lower belly yields to (the domination of) the force of gravity while the upper part negates it. Here, man's 'positive' stand which goes against the force of gravity, is no longer effective. The act of 'straightening up', which denotes an autonomous character, has given way to passivity. This posture, which denies the autonomous character of man, is ugly. *Since* the human being is at the same time a devine being, his bodily form should be noble. To keep the *koshi* erect is indeed the most important outward expression of the soul-body.

Because through wrong posture the upper body must, as it were, sit on a crumpled lower body the muscles of the chest, shoulders, neck, face or head become cramped and it is only a makeshift remedy to loosen the cramp by kneading and massage. To obviate the source of this cramp completely one must straighten the spine and adopt the right posture.

This right posture, which permits the body to maintain its proper perpendicular position, is the only way of attaining that degree of form which demonstrates the unity of life beyond all dualism. One must escape from that imprisonment in the ego which causes cramp in various parts, and then a condition of ego-lessness will arise. But at the edge of the abyss life rushes in again.

A posture in which the lower part of the body is heavy and the upper part light necessarily develops a body structure with a strong *koshi* and a protruding lower belly. If one adopts a right posture the *koshi* becomes as firm as a rock. Then one can do nothing other than put the strength quite naturally into the lower abdomen. This strength tenses the abdominal muscles in a pleasant way and gives vitality to the whole body. The tension of the lower belly is strongest in exhalation, so strong in fact that a fist struck against it will rebound. Hakuin Zenshi, in his book *Yasenkawa*, has compared such a belly with a 'ball that has not yet been hit with a bamboo stick', meaning a ball with unimpaired strength and elasticity.

Tensing the chest, drawing up the muscles, flattening the lower belly—all this shifts the centre of gravity upwards and thus produces instability. The chest should be absolutely empty. One should take care to open and soften and ease the chest, and never to tense it. The whole body-strength should lie exclusively in the *koshi* as the root of the trunk; the muscles of the whole body should naturally tend towards the *koshi*-region. When this region is filled with strength, and when the upper body and the neck are quite free, the movement of any of the limbs—any effort whatsoever—expresses the wholeness and unity centred in the tanden and produces no strain or distortion at any point. Thus every particular movement, which is always somewhere, becomes existentially, a wonderful entity in the nowhere.

When withdrawing the strength from the chest one should at the same time let the pit of the stomach cave in. The pit of the stomach is the concave region below the breastbone and above the navel and the part which is called upper belly in contrast to the lower belly. If one bends the *koshi* this region caves in. One can, however, gather the strength of the whole body in the tanden only when this goes in, even when one holds the koshi erect and tenses the lower belly while exhaling. When inhaling one should breathe in with empty relaxed chest. Then the air fills the upper belly and swells the region above the navel naturally. When exhaling, the muscle-power is concentrated in the lower belly. Then the upper belly caves in naturally as if it were being sucked into a vacuum.

If the *koshi* is the most important region for acquiring right posture, then one could say that the next most important part is the neck. The *koshi* and the neck are the most unstable parts of the body. Therefore, to achieve the right posture, one must keep these two parts in order. The head is joined to the trunk by means of a thin and flexible neck which forms its base. If one holds one's head in the wrong way the actual stem of the whole body will be divided into head and trunk, so that each possesses a separate centre of gravity. This would represent dualism. To achieve the unity of the whole body, one must take care that the centre of gravity of the head is exactly in line with the body-stem. The lower jaw of many people drops forward in a slack way. One must pull the chin in slightly and keep the ear lobes in a straight line with the shoulders. So the masters taught that one should keep the cervical vertebrae straight and put strength into the neck, in fact to pull the chin in so far that 'it hurts behind the ears'. In the right posture the strength one puts into the *koshi* and the strength which pulls in the chin are closely connected. If one loses the strength of the *koshi* the chin falls too far forward.

To put the strength into the neck and to pull in the chin does not mean that one should put the same amount of strength into the latter as into the *koshi* but that one should keep the neck muscles under control. 'If one tries only to pull in the chin paying no attention to the *koshi* and to the pit of the stomach, the chest will involuntarily spring forward' (Okada). When the chest protrudes, the belly muscles are drawn up and the whole musculature of the body is displaced. The strength in the *koshi* dwindles. In this bad posture it is unhealthy to put strength into the lower belly by force. Because the *koshi*, as the base of the trunk is also the seat of the body-whole, the strength put in the neck muscles must combined without difficulty with the strength put into the *koshi*, or to express it differently, one must create from the koshi the strength which keeps the neck muscles in order.

Because in the condition wherein the neck and the trunk are truly one, the cervical muscles undergo neither distortion nor cramp, the head seems almost as if it were 'exploded' from the trunk, as if it hung suspended in empty space. The head is heaven, the trunk is earth. Only where heaven and earth, which are actually one, are divided into a duality within the frame of the one, does a great well-ordered cosmos appear. When the strength of the neck enters that of the tanden and when the head is at one with the whole musculature of the body the head feels as if it were lightly floating no matter which way it moves.

The shoulders are the most mobile part of the trunk. They also distort the whole body most easily. For the practice of right posture the shoulders are the most important part of the body. It is essential to let the shoulders drop. As the head represents Heaven and the trunk Earth the true form of the human body can be represented only when the shoulders are loose and when one drops oneself into the basic centre thus actualizing the true emptiness of Heaven and the fullness of Earth. To draw in the neck and to hunch the shoulders up is to clump the two together thus making them a mere thing, and so falling into a lower dimension of life. Most weak people hold their shoulders hunched-up. When one is frightened or startled one involuntarily jerks up the shoulders. Anyone not thrusting up his shoulders when startled but gathering his strength in his lower belly must certainly have 'practised' in some way.

The cardinal point in relaxing the shoulders is to let them droop gently, as if one were letting a soutane slip off. But if one puts one's consciousness into the shoulders in order to drop them, they will be cramped rather than relaxed. Any part of the body will become tense if one deliberately puts one's consciousness into it. So nothing remains but to put consciousness into the tanden. There one's whole attention can be centred without causing any harm. Therefore, when dropping the shoulders, it is better to have the feeling that one is dropping both arms rather than intending to drop the shoulders. If one puts no strength into the arms whatsoever and feels as if the arms were separated from the shoulders, the shoulder muscles at once become calmer. The calmer the shoulder muscles the calmer the whole body. When the legs also extend calmly downwards and the shoulders are quiet, the chin is then drawn in of its own accord. One can say, therefore, that the most effective approach to correct posture lies in the right dropping of both arms.

Both shoulders must be level and form a straight line when seen from above. In most people, however, the roots of the arms tend backwards at the shoulders. Then one must not only drop the shoulders but, in so doing also arch them forward a little. This is the posture of a Noh dancer as he begins his dance, with arms hanging naturally, the fan in his right hand. The shoulders of a master of archery also form a straight line when he looses his arrow. If in archery one does not let the shoulders sink and does not drop the arms slightly forward the root of the left arm rises and one cannot make the bow-arm strong enough.

The art of a sculptor consists, it is said, in chiselling out of the wood an already existent image. Similarly, to achieve right posture, to extricate man's inherent posture, means to clear away the confused accumulations of misdoing. Therefore one should not be caught by anxious effort to arch forward the lower belly, to drop the shoulders, etc. Rather should one turn one's mind directly to the unity of the whole body, purifying this feeling of oneness from all dross, extinguishing all forces which negate the 'one', and, in this way, actualize the tanden as the 'seat' of unity. But the two efforts, to keep the koshi erect and secondly to drop the arms are different from all the other efforts as they do not divide the mind but are good ways of achieving the overall unity of the body.

When standing upright the force of gravity of the body falls in a plumb line from the crown of the head through its centre down through the trunk emerging between the legs. If one opens the legs at a moderate angle the seat of gravity widens and the degree of stability is increased.

With the koshi not erect the weight of gravity falls on the heels and in this posture a man can easily be pushed over.

If one walks with ease, the body-stem upright, the koshi filled with strength, the leg muscles stretched naturally, the body knows no faltering, to the right or to the left. Then one walks parallel to the surface of the earth as though on a water mirror. Such is the gait of a Noh player. The Noh player learns to walk with a basin of water on his head. That is the right way of walking.

Right sitting reveals the true form of man. As it is said in the *Fugen Sutra*, 'Right sitting and meditating the true form' constitutes the proto-image of any 'practice' of man. Right sitting is itself the true form of man and the full accomplishment of it a primary human experience. The bodily act of right sitting in free self-consciousness is, like other good things, the practice of one among several possible good things as well as in itself a realization of the absolute Unity which transcends all the relative unities. Thus the perfection of a state ultimately possible to man can be brought about merely by the right practice of sitting.

Philosophical thinking practised by a person who has degenerated into a mere brain and whose posture resembles that of a jelly-fish—such thinking remains ultimately in the sphere of illusion and vague phantasies however profound it may appear. Only because the wondrous teaching proclaimed from the golden mouth of the Shaka[1] was spoken from his noble physical body is its truth the expression of experience grounded in Reality.

[1] Sakyamuni (the Buddha).

Chapter 3

Kaneko Shoseki:
Nature and Origin of Man

Kaneko Shoseki had acquired the power of healing after having gained partial enlightenment in March 1910 as the result of many years practice of Zen Buddhism. After years of fruitful work as a healer he lost his miraculous powers and recognized that the reason for this lay in a residuum of pride still remaining in himself. Renewed and deepened turning to inner practice led him to new realizations about the nature of man. His book *Nature and Origin of Man* is a compilation of his new realizations. We give here some extracts related to the theme of this book—Hara.

In the completely degenerated conditions of modern life it has seemed to me urgently necessary to set forth fundamental Reality and so to determine the highest standards of thought, action and faith.

As for the means by which this fundamental Reality is to be grasped I could naturally base nothing on Western thought. I was convinced that it was plainly necessary in such a profound search to begin at an absolute starting point, that is with the abolition of the usual 'relative' methods of research. Therefore I had to follow the ancient Eastern course which had already long ago recognized the necessity of a final and total inner awareness of the eternal Reality. In the conviction that in this way alone the final goal of all essential search might be reached, I set myself to follow the religious practices of the Eastern saints. But the way was long and hard, the goal all too distant from where I stood for my desire to be easily fulfilled. Only my constant striving in *practice*, continued for twenty-two years, allowed me to declare my firm conviction that mankind on the whole has long since forgotten the fundamental law and has been led astray into a non-essential, superficial, in short, an externalized way of living. I am afraid that with this assertion I have unfortunately to go against those many eminent thinkers and educators who are at present highly honoured in the world. But I shall speak of what I found to be certain and right, confirmed by the experiences and insights gained from treating many sufferers who have asked my help to deliver them from illness and sorrow. All men carry within them in body and soul inherited sins as well as a tendency to sins and delusions of every kind—the life-and-soul-destroying devil which cannot be driven out except by the appropriate religious practice.

If the Absolute exists for us at all it must in some way be experienced by us as evident Reality, just as material objects are perceived by our senses. And for this there is only one way—to make a clean sweep of 'scientific thinking' and to let the mind root itself in our innermost being. Whatever is presented to the merely outward I, not permeated by Being, is of only relative certainty.

True knowledge of the Absolute becomes possible only when its existence is experienced, not merely as a theoretical necessity, but when it is felt personally within our own innermost being. This Something so experienced is what I call the unquestionable creative rhythm of the life force, or the fundamental law of God which rules the whole world, and also that which gives us the highest standard of value by which to measure all our experiences. Only by this personal assurance can we free ourselves from the sins and delusions hidden in our bodies and minds and so become citizens of the Kingdom of Heaven. Philosophers, theologians, artists and moralists, generally speaking, attempt to find truth but until they have grasped that Something in personal experience their efforts will never cease to be a groping in the dark and will produce results of only superficial worth.

Original truth reveals itself only when one gives up all preconceived ideas. No suppositions, no theoretical thinking, no ideal concepts are helpful. All these will only confuse the soul in pursuit of an ever elusive Being and in the end he will have to confess with a sigh that all his striving has been meaningless and vain and that he would do better to live happily in modest ignorance than to be burdened with a really useless load of much-knowing. But all this is a fore-doomed tragedy which will never end until we know how to eradicate the roots of 'Original Sin' by deep practice. In my opinion the Primordial is the essence or ground of the whole man, and the ordinary ego with its greed for so-called objective knowledge is only the superstructure.

The understanding of the law of harmony must necessarily be preceded by the discovery of its centre of gravity. As every single physical object has its centre of gravity so the human body also must have its centre of gravity. In man it is the tanden, the centre of the body where the Primordial has its seat. This is the most important fundamental fact and all anthropological research must proceed from a proved inner assurance of it.

If one concentrates all the activities of the mind which are normally directed outward, that is, ideas, judgments, feelings, volitions and even the function of breathing, in fact if all the life energy is concentrated in the centre of the body, in the tanden, a new sphere of consciousness arises within us which completely transcends the opposition of objective and subjective, of outward and inward and even our usual vague sleep-clouded consciousness. This leads to the absolute and final stage of spiritual experience in which one realizes that God himself lives and works as the highest principle and the Primordial Source of life in every single being, as well as in Nature as a whole. That which reigns in the individual as the unmediated administrator of the Divine Law within every human being is what I call the 'primordial I' or the original One. For it is not only that from which all man's activity, whether conscious or unconscious, proceeds, but also it is the one thing in man which belongs completely and directly to the highest Being. Realization of this is the deepest experience which the human mind can reach.

To every activity of body as well as of mind the function of breathing stands in the closest relationship, a relationship which is not only a physiological one but an immediate essential one. For between the original One and the external ego there are two connecting links, namely breathing and the system of the 14 *keiraku.*

By *keiraku* I mean those imperceptible fine passages in the body which connect bones, muscles, brain, intestines, the senses, etc. with each other and eventually reconnect them all with the primal Life Force. Like the blood vessels and nerve fibres connecting all the inner organs they run through the whole body, mostly alongside the blood vessels. But in relation to their function the keiraku are quite different—their function is in the nature of supervising the circulation of blood and the movement of thought and allowing each individual organ to work harmoniously with all the others. They neither nourish the organs nor are they controlled by the brain. They are so to speak a network of passages which transmits to all parts of the body the spiritual-physical rhythm of the Life Force. Thus the *keiraku* together with the Life Force, which unites them in itself, are the only parts of man which belong unqualifiedly to the universal Life. Furthermore we can apprehend them by this—that in death they disappear completely, that no trace of their existence can be found in a corpse. They can be detected only when the ordinary I is on the point of returning to its normal consciousness after the absolute state of Illumination. They are then perceived inwardly as the flow of an ethereal primal force. They cannot be discovered by an objective examination from without.

It is on the depth and fineness of the breath and on the perfect functioning of the keiraku that the closeness of their relationship depends. Only through calm deep breathing can the primal Life Force preserve its actual function in rhythm with the eternal Being, while the *keiraku* receives its power and transmits it to each separate part of the body. This is the essential condition not only for perfect health but also for true knowledge. From the start, certainly, man must have had the Primordial implanted in him. But because of the ever growing tendency towards an externalized and conceptual way of living and thinking and the often complete shifting of the centre of fundamental life values to objectified values, it happens that breathing, which at all times should be deep and subtle, becomes gradually shallower and coarser until it can no longer reach the lower belly. If once such a tendency has become established in our bodies the Primordial loses its power, the *keiraku* grow stronger in one part, weaker in others, and the whole person then stands beyond the influence of the primordial Life Force. It is self-evident that a merely idealistic approach can do little for the restoration of the individual as a whole. Modern man has degenerated *essentially*, that is, not only rationally and morally but substantively. There is only one way to essential salvation and that is by the appropriate inner religious practice. It is a simple understandable thing that since the cause of all degeneration such as illness, suffering, delusion and stupidity is the separation of man's mind from his being, it is only necessary to join the two together again.

Practice every day, let go all your fixed notions and feelings, indeed let go completely your present I. When through long serious practice you shed all preconceptions, become inwardly clear and empty you will gradually be able to delay exhalation for quite a long while and to retain the breath in the lower belly deeply and quietly. When this happens the strain of wrong effort will gradually ease, inner perception will grow clearer and in the tanden you will feel a source of strength never before experienced—the Original Source.

Apart from the normal communication between men through language and action there is another quite different sort of mutual influence. It is that of the rhythm of the Original strength which permeates all human beings and all Nature. Through it every individual thing in essence and, as it were, underground, is connected with every other. If then one who is further removed from the working of the Primordial Force is close to one who lives more in accord with it, the rhythm of the Primordial Force will certainly be transmitted from the one to the other. The latter without knowing it exerts a good influence on the former.

The relation between artistic creation and the tanden, the seat of the Primordial, is immediate and essential. Neither the hand nor the head should paint the picture. It is a necessary condition for the expression of the essential in all art that the artist should empty and free his head, and then concentrate his whole energy in the tanden. His brush will then move of itself in accord with the rhythm of the Primordial Force. If, on the contrary, in drawing the lines he uses the strength of his hand, or if he works under personal tension, what he wants to express will be cut off from the source of inner synthesis, and will look hard and fixed.

The synthesis as the oneness of subject and object does not have to be 'produced', it is there underlying the reality. And only through this complete knowledge can it be brought to light. This must be a whole, an all-human knowledge which has its place neither in the head nor in the

heart but in the centre of the whole person. What belongs
to the head or the heart alone is really peripheral and
therefore remote from Being.

The Primordial although it is in-dwelling in man's
deepest being does not in any way belong to him for it is
universal and only loaned to him by the highest Being.
Therefore our minds and bodies and our very lives, through
the primordial Life Force, are dependent on the Absolute.
We owe our whole existence never to ourselves but always
to the Absolute. We ourselves are nothing; as nothing we
belong to the Absolute.

When the Primal Force, ever working gradually within
us, finally reaches the highest peak of its activity then out of
the thick heavy fog of ordinary consciousness there bursts
forth from the eternal Being the clearest possible state of
consciousness—the one we have designated as the absolute
and final degree of human experience. Here no fixed form
is perceptible, neither an object nor an I, neither an inner
nor an outer, breathing is suspended, the bodily shell
completely vanished. Here no body exists, no mind, neither
man nor world. The ego is completely at one with the
world. What alone reigns in this experience is Universal.

The primal Force of Life, exactly like water rushing
swiftly through a tube, streams from eternity to eternity
whirling around in the lower part of one's body.

The living recognition of our absolute dependence on the
highest Being is the perfect phenomenon of ultimate self-
awareness. In the beginning man lost his Paradise through
becoming conscious of himself. He can regain it only by
achieving self-consciousness anew.